500+ JAVA & J2EE Interview Q & A

(Core Java, Advance Java, Servlet, JSP, EJB, JMS, JDBC, JNDI)

By Bandana Ojha

Table of Content

Introduction

The authors of this Java and J2EE book has conducted so many Java/J2EEinterviews at various companies and meticulously collected the most effective java j2ee interview notes with simple, straightforward explanations. Rather than going through comprehensive, textbook-sized java j2ee reference guides, this book includes only the information required immediately for java j2ee interview to start their career in java j2ee platform. Answers of all the questions are short and to the point. It includes core Java, Servlet, JSP, EJB, JMS, JDCC, JNDB, This Java J2EE interview book contains 500+ questions and answers and we assure that you will get 90% frequently asked Java J2EE interview questions going through this book. It will clear your core java fundamentals, concepts and boost your confidence to appear any Java J2EE interview in any companies anywhere in the world whether it is telephonic or face to face.

Good luck to ALL!!!

Core & Advance Java

1.What's the base class in Java from which all classes are derived?

java.lang.object is the base class in java from which all classes are derived.

2.What's the difference between an array and Vector?

An array groups data of same primitive type and is static in nature while vectors are dynamic in nature and can hold data of different data types.

3.Is there a way to increase the size of an array after its declaration?

Arrays are static and once we have specified its size, we can't change it. If we want to use such collections where we may require a change of size (no of items), we should prefer vector over array.

4.What is immutable class? Can you write immutable object?

Immutable classes are Java classes whose objects cannot be modified once created. Any modification in Immutable object result in new object. For example, String is immutable in Java. Mostly Immutable are also final in Java, to prevent sub class from overriding methods in Java which can compromise Immutability. You can achieve same functionality by making member as non-final but private and not modifying them except in constructor.

5. What is the difference between factory and abstract factory pattern?

Abstract Factory provides one more level of abstraction. Consider different factories each extended from an Abstract

Factory and responsible for creation of different hierarchies of objects based on the type of factory.
E.g. AbstractFactory extended
by AutomobileFactory, UserFactory, RoleFactory etc. Each individual factory would be responsible for creation of objects in that genre.

6. Can you override private or static method in Java?

No, you cannot override private or static method in Java, if you create similar method with same return type and same method arguments that's called method hiding.

7. What is the difference between continue and break statement?

Break and continue are two important keywords used in Loops. When a break keyword is used in a loop, loop is broken instantly while when continue keyword is used, current iteration is broken, and loop continues with next iteration.

8. Can main () method in Java can return any data?

In java, main () method can't return any data and hence, it's always declared with a void return type.

9. How can we pass argument to a function by reference instead of pass by value?

In java, we can pass argument to a function only by value and not by reference.

10. Can a class have multiple constructors?

Yes, a class can have multiple constructors with different parameters. Which constructor gets used for object creation depends on the arguments passed while creating the objects.

11. Is String a data type in java?

String is not a primitive data type in java. When a string is created in java, it's an object of Java.Lang. String class that gets created. After creation of this string object, all built-in methods of String class can be used on the string object.

12. What's difference between Stack and Queue?

Stack and Queue both are used as placeholder for a collection of data. The primary difference between a stack and a queue is that stack is based on Last in First out (LIFO) principle while a queue is based on FIFO (First in First Out) principle.

13. Describe different states of a thread.

A thread in Java can be in either of the following states:

Ready: When a thread is created, it's in Ready state.

Running: A thread currently being executed is in running state.

Waiting: A thread waiting for another thread to free certain resources is in waiting state.

Dead: A thread which has gone dead after execution is in dead state.

14. Can we call a non-static method from a static method?

Non-Static methods are owned by objects of a class and have object level scope and to call the non-Static methods from a static block (like from a static main method), an object of the class needs to be created first. Then using object reference, these methods can be invoked.

15. Can a dead thread be started again?

In java, a thread which is in dead state can't be started again. There is no way to restart a dead thread.

16. What's the difference between comparison done by equals method and == operator?

In Java, equals () method is used to compare the contents of two string objects and returns true if the two have same value while == operator compares the references of two string objects.

In the following example, equals () returns true as the two string objects have same values. However, == operator returns false as both string objects are referencing to different objects:

17. What is the difference between double and float variables in Java?

In java, float takes 4 bytes in memory while Double takes 8 bytes in memory. Float is single precision floating point decimal number while Double is double precision decimal number.

18. What is Final Keyword in Java? Give an example.

In java, a constant is declared using the keyword Final. Value can be assigned only once and after assignment, value of a constant can't be changed.

In below example, a constant with the name const_val is declared and assigned a value:

Private Final int const_val=10

When a method is declared as final, it can NOT be overridden by the subclasses. This method is faster than any other method, because they are resolved at complied time.

When a class is declaring as final, it cannot be sub classed. Example String, Integer and other wrapper classes.

19. What are Java Packages? What's the significance of packages?

In Java, package is a collection of classes and interfaces which are bundled together as they are related to each other. Use of packages helps developers to modularize the code and group the code for proper re-use. Once code has been packaged in Packages, it can be imported in other classes and used.

20. Does Importing a package imports its sub-packages as well in Java?

In java, when a package is imported, its sub-packages aren't imported, and developer needs to import them separately if required.

For example, if a developer imports a package college. *, all classes in the package named college are loaded but no classes from the sub-package are loaded. To load the classes from its sub-package (say library), developer must import it explicitly as follows:

Import college. library. *

21. How objects of a class are created if no constructor is defined in the class?

Even if no explicit constructor is defined in a java class, objects get created successfully as a default constructor is implicitly used for object creation. This constructor has no parameters.

22. What's the benefit of using inheritance?

Key benefit of using inheritance is reusability of code as inheritance enables sub-classes to reuse the code of its super class. Polymorphism (Extensibility) is another great benefit which allow new functionality to be introduced without effecting existing derived classes.

23. What's the default access specifier for variables and methods of a class?

Default access specifier for variables and method is package protected i.e. variables and class is available to any other class but in the same package, not outside the package.

24. What's difference between Stack and Queue?

Stack and Queue both are used as placeholder for a collection of data. The primary difference between a stack and a queue is that stack is based on Last in First out (LIFO) principle while a queue is based on FIFO (First In First Out) principle.

25. How can we use primitive data types as objects?

Primitive data types like int can be handled as objects using their respective wrapper classes. For example, Integer is a wrapper class for primitive data type int. We can apply different methods to a wrapper class, just like any other object.

26. Which types of exceptions are caught at compile time?

Checked exceptions can be caught at the time of program compilation. Checked exceptions must be handled by using try catch block in the code to successfully compile the code.

27. What are the two environment variables that must be set to run any Java programs?

Java programs can be executed in a machine only once following two environment variables have been properly set:

PATH variable

CLASSPATH variable

28. Is JDK required on each machine to run a Java program?

JDK is development Kit of Java and is required for development only and to run a Java program on a machine, JDK isn't required. Only JRE is required.

29. What is the difference between an Inner Class and a Sub-Class?

An Inner class is a class which is nested within another class. An Inner class has access rights for the class which is nesting it and it can access all variables and methods defined in the outer class.

A sub-class is a class which inherits from another class called super class. Sub-class can access all public and protected methods and fields of its super class.

30. What is data encapsulation and what's its significance?

Encapsulation is a concept in Object Oriented Programming for combining properties and methods in a single unit.

Encapsulation helps programmers to follow a modular approach for software development as each object has its own set of methods and variables and serves its functions independent of other objects. Encapsulation also serves data hiding purpose.

31. What are the performance implications of Interfaces over abstract classes?

Interfaces are slower in performance as compared to abstract classes as extra indirections are required for interfaces. Another key factor for developers to take into consideration is that any class can extend only one abstract class while a class can implement many interfaces.

Use of interfaces also puts an extra burden on the developers as any time an interface is implemented in a class; developer is forced to implement every method of interface.

32. Why Strings in Java are called as Immutable?

In java, string objects are called immutable as once value has been assigned to a string, it can't be changed and if changed, a new object is created.

33. What is multi-threading?

Multi-threading is a programming concept to run multiple tasks in a concurrent manner within a single program. Threads share same process stack and running in parallel. It helps in performance improvement of any program.

34. Can a variable be local and static at the same time?

No, a variable can't be static as well as local at the same time. Defining a local variable as static gives compilation error.

35. I want to re-reach and use an object once it has been garbage collected. How it's possible?

Once an object has been destroyed by garbage collector, it no longer exists on the heap and it can't be accessed again. There is no way to reference it again.

36. What is the difference between creating String as new () and literal?

When we create string with new () Operator, it's created in heap and not added into string pool while String created using literal are created in String pool itself which exists in PermGen area of heap.

String s = new String("Test");

does not put the object in String pool, we need to call String.intern() method which is used to put them into String pool explicitly. its only when you create String object as String literal e.g. String s = "Test" Java automatically put that into String pool.

37. What is difference between StringBuffer and StringBuilder in Java?

String Builder in Java is introduced in Java 5 and only difference between both is that String buffer methods
are synchronized while StringBuilder is a non-synchronized.

38. What is the difference between Executor submit () and Executor execute () method?

There is a difference when looking at exception handling. If your tasks throw an exception and if it was submitted
with execute this exception will go to the uncaught exception handler (when you don't have provided one explicitly, the default one will just print the stack trace to System. Error). If you submitted the task with submit any thrown
exception, checked exception or not, is then part of the task's return status. For a task that was submitted with submit and that terminates with an exception, the Future get will re-throw this exception, wrapped in an ExecutionException.

39. What is difference between JDK, JRE and JVM?

JVM: JVM is an acronym for Java Virtual Machine, it is an abstract machine which provides the runtime environment in which java bytecode can be executed. It is a specification.

JVMs are available for many hardware and software platforms (so JVM is platform dependent).

JRE: JRE stands for Java Runtime Environment. It is the implementation of JVM.

JDK: JDK is an acronym for Java Development Kit. It physically exists. It contains JRE + development tools.

40. What is platform?

A platform is basically the hardware or software environment in which a program runs. There are two types of platforms software-based and hardware-based. Java provides software-based platform.

41. What is the main difference between Java platform and other platforms?

The Java platform differs from most other platforms in the sense that it's a software-based platform that runs on top of other hardware-based platforms. It has two components:

Runtime Environment

API (Application Programming Interface)

42. What if I write static public void instead of public static void?

Program compiles and runs properly.

43. What is difference between object-oriented programming language and object-based programming language?

Object based programming languages follow all the features of OOPs except Inheritance. Examples of object-based programming languages are JavaScript, VBScript etc.

44. Can you make a constructor final?

No, constructor can't be final.

45. Which class is the superclass for every class.

Object class.is the super class of every class.

46.What is composition?

Holding the reference of the other class within some other class is known as composition.

47. Why Java does not support pointers?

Pointer is a variable that refers to the memory address. They are not used in java because they are unsafe(unsecured) and complex to understand.

48. Can we override static method?

No, you can't override the static method because they are the part of class not object.

49. Why we cannot override static method?

It is because the static method is the part of class and it is bound with class whereas instance method is bound with object and static gets memory in class area and instance gets memory in heap.

50. Difference between method Overloading and Overriding.

Method Overloading:

Method overloading increases the readability of the program.

method overloading occurs within the class.

In this case, parameter must be different.

Method Overriding:

Method overriding provides the specific implementation of the method that is already provided by its super class.

method overloading occurs within two the classes.

In this case, parameter must be same.

51. Can there be any abstract method without abstract class?

No, if there is any abstract method in a class, that class must be abstract.

52. Can you use abstract and final both with a method?

No, because abstract method needs to be overridden whereas you can't override final method.

53. Is it possible to instantiate the abstract class?

No, abstract class can never be instantiated.

54. Can you declare an interface method static?

No, because methods of an interface are abstract by default, and static and abstract keywords can't be used together.

55. Can an Interface be final?

No, because its implementation is provided by another class.

56. What is marker interface?

An interface that have no data member and method is known as a marker interface. For example, Serializable, Cloneable etc.

57. Can we define private and protected modifiers for variables in interfaces?

No, they are implicitly public.

58.When can an object reference be cast to an interface reference?

An object reference can be cast to an interface reference when the object implements the referenced interface.

59. Do I need to import java. lang package?

No. It is by default loaded internally by the JVM.

60. Can I import same package/class twice? Will the JVM load the package twice at runtime?

One can import the same package or same class multiple times. Neither compiler nor JVM complains about it. But the JVM will internally load the class only once no matter how many times you import the same class.

61. What is difference between Checked Exception and Unchecked Exception?

Checked Exception:

The classes that extend Throwable class except RuntimeException and Error are known as checked exceptions e.g. IOException, SQLException etc. Checked exceptions are checked at compile-time.

Unchecked Exception:

The classes that extend RuntimeException are known as unchecked exceptions e.g. Arithmetic Exception, NullPointerException etc. Unchecked exceptions are not checked at compile-time.

62. What is the base class for Error and Exception?

Throwable.is the base class for error and exceptions.

63. Is it necessary that each try block must be followed by a catch block?

It is not necessary that each try block must be followed by a catch block. It should be followed by either a catch block OR a finally block. And whatever exceptions are likely to be thrown should be declared in the throws clause of the method.

64. What is difference between throw and throws?

throw keyword:

throw is used to explicitly throw an exception.

checked exceptions cannot be propagated with throw only

throw is followed by an instance.

throw is used within the method.

You cannot throw multiple exception

throws keyword:

throws is used to declare an exception.

checked exception can be propagated with throws.

throws is followed by class.

throws is used with the method signature.

You can declare multiple exception e.g. public void method()throws IOException, SQLException.

65. What is the meaning of immutable in terms of String?

The simple meaning of immutable is unmodifiable or unchangeable. Once string object has been created, its value can't be changed.

66. Why string objects are immutable in java?

Because java uses the concept of string literal. Suppose there are 5 reference variables, all refers to one object "John". If one reference variable changes the value of the object, it will be affected to all the reference variables. That is why string objects are immutable in java.

67. What is the basic difference between string and string buffer object?

String is an immutable object. StringBuffer is a mutable object.

68. What is the purpose of toString() method in java?

The toString() method returns the string representation of any object. If you print any object, java compiler internally invokes the toString() method on the object. So, overriding the toString() method, returns the desired output, it can be the state of an object etc. depends on your implementation.

69. What is Garbage Collection?

Garbage collection is a process of reclaiming the runtime unused objects. It is performed for memory management.

70. What is gc()?

gc() is a daemon thread.gc() method is defined in System class that is used to send request to JVM to perform garbage collection.

71.What is difference between final, finally and finalize ()?

final: final is a keyword, final can be variable, method or class. You, can't change the value of final variable, can't override final method, can't inherit final class.

finally: finally block is used in exception handling. finally block is always executed.

finalize(): finalize() method is used in garbage collection. finalize() method is invoked just before

72. What is the difference between notify() and notifyAll()?

The notify() is used to unblock one waiting thread whereas notifyAll() method is used to unblock all the threads in waiting state.

73. What is deadlock?

Deadlock is a situation when two threads are waiting on each other to release a resource. Each thread waiting for a resource which is held by the other waiting thread.

74. What is the difference between ArrayList and LinkedList?

ArrayList

ArrayList uses a dynamic array.

ArrayList is not efficient for manipulation because a lot of shifting is required.

ArrayList is better to store and fetch data.

LinkedList

LinkedList uses doubly linked list.

LinkedList is efficient for manipulation.

LinkedList is better to manipulate data.

75. What is the difference between Set and Map?

Set contains values only whereas Map contains key and values both.

76. What is the difference between Collection and Collections?

Collection is an interface whereas Collections is a class. Collection interface provides normal functionality of data structure to List, Set and Queue. But, Collections class is to sort and synchronize collection elements.

77. What are the steps to connect to the database in java?

Registering the driver class

Creating connection

Creating statement

Executing queries

Closing connection

78. How can we store and retrieve images from the database?

By using Prepared Statement interface, we can store and retrieve images.

79. Can we declare a class as Abstract without having any abstract method?

Yes, we can create an abstract class by using abstract keyword before class name even if it doesn't have any abstract method. However, if a class has even one abstract method, it must be declared as abstract otherwise it will give an error.

80. What's the difference between an Abstract Class and Interface in Java?

The primary difference between an abstract class and interface is that an interface can only possess declaration of public static methods with no concrete implementation while an abstract class can have members with any access specifiers (public, private etc.) with or without concrete implementation.

Another key difference in the use of abstract classes and interfaces is that a class which implements an interface must implement all the methods of the interface while a class which inherits from an abstract class doesn't require implementation of all the methods of its super class.

A class can implement multiple interfaces, but it can extend only one abstract class.

81. Can a class have multiple constructors?

Yes, a class can have multiple constructors with different parameters. Which constructor gets used for object creation depends on the arguments passed while creating the objects.

82. Can we override static methods of a class?

We cannot override static methods. Static methods belong to a class and not to individual objects and are resolved at the time of compilation (not at runtime). Even if we try to override static method, we will not get a compilation error, nor the impact of overriding when running the code.

83. Why Runnable Interface is used in Java?

Runnable interface is used in java for implementing multi-threaded applications. Java.Lang. Runnable interface is implemented by a class to support multi-threading.

84. What are the two ways of implementing multi-threading in Java?

Multi-threaded applications can be developed in Java by using any of the following two methodologies:

By using Java. Lang. Runnable Interface. Classes implement this interface to enable multi-threading. There is a Run() method in this interface which is implemented.

By writing a class that extend Java.Lang. Thread class.

85. There are two classes named class A and class B. Both classes are in the same package. Can a private member of class A can be accessed by an object of class B?

Private members of a class aren't accessible outside the scope of that class and any other class even in the same package can't access them.

86. Is it correct to say that due to garbage collection feature in Java, a java program never goes out of memory?

Even though automatic garbage collection is provided by Java, it doesn't ensure that a Java program will not go out of memory as there is a possibility that creation of Java objects is being done at a faster pace compared to garbage collection resulting in filling of all the available memory resources.

So, garbage collection helps in reducing the chances of a program going out of memory, but it doesn't ensure that.

87. Can we have any other return type than void for main method?

No, Java class main method can have only void return type for the program to get successfully executed.

Nonetheless, if you absolutely must return a value to at the completion of main method, you can use System.exit(int status)

88. I want my class to be developed in such a way that no other class (even derived class) can create its objects. How can I do so?

If we declare the constructor of a class as private, it will not be accessible by any other class and hence, no other class will be able to instantiate it and formation of its object will be limited to itself only.

89. How objects are stored in Java?

In java, each object when created gets a memory space from a heap. When an object is destroyed by a garbage collector, the space allocated to it from the heap is re-allocated to the heap and becomes available for any new objects.

90. How can we find the actual size of an object on the heap?

In java, there is no way to find out the exact size of an object on the heap.

91. Which API is provided by Java for operations on set of objects?

Java provides a Collection API which provides many useful methods which can be applied on a set of objects. Some of the important classes provided by Collection API include ArrayList, HashMap, TreeSet and TreeMap.

92. What's the base class of all exception classes?

In Java, Java. Lang. Throwable is the super class of all exception classes and all exception classes are derived from this base class.

93. What's the order of call of constructors in inheritance?

In case of inheritance, when a new object of a derived class is created, first the constructor of the super class is invoked and then the constructor of the derived class is invoked.

94. Can we cast any other type to Boolean Type with type casting?

No, we can neither cast any other primitive type to Boolean data type nor can cast Boolean data type to any other primitive data type.

95. Can we use a default constructor of a class even if an explicit constructor is defined?

Java provides a default no argument constructor if no explicit constructor is defined in a Java class. But if an explicit constructor has been defined, default constructor can't be invoked, and developer can use only those constructors which are defined in the class.

96. In multi-threading how can we ensure that a resource isn't used by multiple threads simultaneously?

In multi-threading, access to the resources which are shared among multiple threads can be controlled by using the concept of synchronization. Using synchronized keyword, we can ensure that only one thread can use shared resource at a time and others can get control of the resource only once it has become free from the other one using it.

97. What are the various access specifiers for Java classes?

In Java, access specifiers are the keywords used before a class name which defines the access scope. The types of access specifiers for classes are:

1. Public: Class, Method, Field is accessible from anywhere.

2. Protected: Method, Field can be accessed from the same class to which they belong or from the sub-classes, and from the class of same package, but not from outside.

3. Default: Method, Field, class can be accessed only from the same package and not from outside of its native package.

4. Private: Method, Field can be accessed from the same class to which they belong.

98. What's the purpose of Static methods and static variables?

When there is a requirement to share a method or a variable between multiple objects of a class instead of creating separate copies for each object, we use static keyword to make a method or variable shared for all objects.

99. What is a singleton class? Give a practical example of its usage.

A singleton class in java can have only one instance and hence all its methods and variables belong to just one instance. Singleton class concept is useful for the situations when there is a need to limit the number of objects for a class.

The best example of singleton usage scenario is when there is a limit of having only one connection to a database due to some driver limitations or because of any licensing issues.

100. How can you generate random numbers in Java?

Using Math.random() you can generate random numbers in the range 0.1 to 1.0

Using Random class in package java.util

101.Is constructor inherited?

No, constructor is not inherited.

102. Can we declare the main method of our class as private?

In java, main method must be public static to run any application correctly. If main method is declared as private, developer won't get any compilation error however, it will not get executed and will give a runtime error.

103. Is it compulsory for a Try Block to be followed by a Catch Block in Java for Exception handling?

Try block needs to be followed by either Catch block or Finally block or both. Any exception thrown from try block needs to be either caught in the catch block or else any specific tasks to be performed before code abortion are put in the Finally block.

104. What's the purpose of using Break in each case of Switch Statement?

Break is used after each case (except the last one) in a switch so that code breaks after the valid case and doesn't flow in the proceeding cases too.

If break isn't used after each case, all cases after the valid case also get executed resulting in wrong results.

105. In Java programming, which method is a must implementation for all threads?

Run() is a method of Runnable interface that must be implemented by all threads.

106. If an application has multiple classes in it, is it okay to have a main method in more than one class?

If there is main method in more than one classes in a java application, it won't cause any issue as entry point for any application will be a specific class and code will start from the main method of that class only.

107. What is difference between wait and notify in Java?

Both wait and notify methods are used for inner thread communication, where wait is used to pause the thread on a condition and notify is used to send notification to waiting threads. Both must be called from synchronized context e.g. synchronized method or block.

108. Difference between Serializable and Externalizable in Java?

Serializable is a marker interface with no methods defined it but Externalizable interface has two methods defined on it e.g. readExternal() and writeExternal() which allows you to control the serialization process. Serializable uses default serialization process which can be very slow for some application.

109. Difference between Association, Composition and Aggregation?

Between association, composition and aggregation, composition is strongest. If part can exist without whole than relationship between two class is known as aggregation but if part cannot exist without whole than relationship between two class is known as composition. Between Inheritance and composition, later provides more flexible design.

110. Difference between private, public, package and protected in Java?

All four are access modifier in Java but only private, public and protected are modifier keyword. There is no keyword for package access, its default in Java. Which means if you don't specify any access modifier than by default that will be accessible inside the same package. Private variables are only accessible in the class they are declared, protected are accessible inside all classes in same package but only on sub class outside package and public variables e.g. method, class or variables are accessible anywhere. This is highest level of access modifier and provide lowest form of encapsulation.

111. What is difference between Iterator and Enumeration in Java?

Main difference is that Iterator was introduced in place of Enumeration. It also allows you to remove elements from collection while traversing which was not possible with Enumeration. The methods of Iterator e.g. hasNext() and next() are also more concise then corresponding methods in Enumeration e.g. hasMoreElements(). You should always use Iterator in your Java code as Enumeration may get deprecated and removed in future Java release.

112. What is difference between Overloading and Overriding in Java?

Though both overloading and overriding are related with methods of same names, but they have different characteristics e.g. Overloaded methods must have different method signature than original method, but overridden method must have same signature. Also, overloaded methods are resolved at compiled time while overridden methods are resolved at runtime. See the detailed answer for more analysis and differences.

113. What is difference between PATH and CLASSPATH in Java

PATH is an environment variable which points to Java binary which is used to run Java programs. CLASSPATH is another environment variable which points to Java class files or JAR files. If a class is not found in CLASSPATH then Java throws ClassNotFoundException.

114. What is difference between Checked and Unchecked Exception in Java?

Checked exception ensures that handling of exception is provided and its verified by compiler also, while for throwing unchecked exception no special provision is needed e.g. throws clause. A method can throw unchecked exception without any throw clause.

115. What gives Java its 'write once and run anywhere' nature?

The bytecode. Java is compiled to be a byte code which is the intermediate language between source code and machine code. This byte code is not platform specific and hence can be fed to any platform.

116. What is classloader in java?

The Java Classloader is a part of the Java Runtime Environment that dynamically loads Java classes into the Java Virtual Machine. Usually classes are only loaded on demand.
The Java run time system does not need to know about files and file systems because of classloaders.

117. What is the default value of the local variables in java?

For numbers, the default value is 0; for Booleans, it is false; and for object references, it is null.

118. What is constructor in java?

A constructor in Java is a block of code like a method that's called when an instance of an object is created. Here are the key differences between a constructor and a method:
A constructor doesn't have a return type. ... Unlike methods, constructors are not considered members of a class.

119. What is the purpose of default constructor in java?

When we do not explicitly define a constructor for a class, then java creates default constructor for the class. It is essentially a non-parameterized constructor, i.e. it doesn't accept any arguments. The default constructor's job is to call the super class constructor and initialize all instance variables.

120. Why main method is static in java?

This is necessary because main() is called by the JVM before any objects are made. Since it is static it can be directly invoked via the class. Similarly, we use static sometime for user defined methods so that we need not to make objects. void indicates that the main() method being declared does not return a value.

121. What is inheritance in java?

Inheritance refers to a feature of Java programming that lets you create classes that are derived from other classes. A class that's based on another class inherits the other class. The class that is inherited is the parent class, the base class, or the superclass.

122. What is method overloading in java?

If a class has multiple methods having same name but different in parameters, it is known as Method Overloading.

123. What is method overriding in java?

If subclass (child class) has the same method as declared in the parent class, it is known as method overriding in java.

In other words, if subclass provides the specific implementation of the method that has been provided by one of its parent class, it is known as method overriding.

124. What is Runtime Polymorphism?

Runtime polymorphism or dynamic method dispatch is a process in which a call to an overridden method is resolved at runtime rather than at compile-time.

In this process, an overridden method is called through the reference variable of a super class. The determination of the method to be called is based on the object being referred to by the reference variable.

125. What is abstraction?

Abstraction is a process of hiding the implementation details and showing only functionality to the user.

126. What is the difference between abstraction and encapsulation?

Abstraction hides the implementation details whereas encapsulation wraps code and data into a single unit.

127. What is Exception Handling?

An exception (or exceptional event) is a problem that arises during the execution of a program. When an Exception occurs the normal flow of the program is disrupted, and the program/Application terminates abnormally, which is not recommended, therefore, these exceptions are to be handled.

Exception Handling is a mechanism to handle runtime errors. It is mainly used to handle checked exceptions.

128. What is exception propagation?

Forwarding the exception object to the invoking method is known as exception propagation.

129. how can we create immutable class in java?

To create immutable class in java, you must do following steps.

Declare the class as final so it can't be extended.

Make all fields private so that direct access is not allowed.

Don't provide setter methods for variables

Make all mutable fields final so that its value can be assigned only once.

Initialize all the fields via a constructor performing deep copy.

Perform cloning of objects in the getter methods to return a copy rather than returning the actual object reference.

130. What is nested class?

A class which is declared inside another class is known as nested class. There are 4 types of nested class member inner class, local inner class, anonymous inner class and static nested class.

131. What is nested interface?

Any interface i.e. declared inside the interface or class, is known as nested interface. It is static by default.

132.What is the difference between Serializable and Externalizable interface?

Serializable is a marker interface but Externalizable is not a marker interface. When you use Serializable interface, your class is serialized automatically by default. But you can override writeObject() and readObject() two methods to control more complex object serialization process. When you use Externalizable interface, you have a complete control over your class's serialization process

133. What is thread in java?

A thread, in the context of Java, is the path followed when executing a program. All Java programs have at least one thread, known as the main thread, which is created by the JVM at the program's start, when the main() method is invoked with the main thread.

134.What is multithreading in java?

Multithreading in java is a process of executing multiple threads simultaneously.

Thread is basically a lightweight sub-process, a smallest unit of processing. Multiprocessing and multithreading, both are used to achieve multitasking.

But we use multithreading than multiprocessing because threads share a common memory area. They don't allocate separate memory area so saves memory, and context-switching between the threads takes less time than process.

Java Multithreading is mostly used in games, animation etc.

135. What does join() method do?

The join() method waits for a thread to die. In other words, it causes the currently running threads to stop executing until the thread it joins with completes its task.

136. Can we use multiple main method in same class?

you can't have more than one main method (String [] args as arguments) within same class.

137. What is deadlock situation in java?

Deadlock describes a situation where two or more threads are blocked forever, waiting for each other. Deadlock occurs when multiple threads need the same locks but obtain them in different order. A Java multithreaded program may suffer from the deadlock condition because the synchronized keyword causes the executing thread to block while waiting for the lock, or monitor, associated with the specified object.

139. How to prevent deadlock?

The problem discussed before can be avoided by applying a suitable deadlock prevention technique. Following are some techniques available that help mitigate the deadlock problem:

Non-Overlapping Locks

Lock Ordering

Lock Timeout

Single Thread

140. How does java platform is different from another platform?

The primary difference between Java and other platforms is that, Java contains JVM (Java virtual machine) and Java API that run on top of other hardware-based platforms. The JVM converts Java code to machine language.

Other benefits that Java has over other platforms include:

Java is a software only platform, whereas other platforms can be hardware only or a hardware software platform.

Java runs on top of hardware platform, whereas other platforms could have only the hardware component.

The Java API supports the writing of Java files, which are then converted to class file, i.e. byte stream by the java compiler.

JVM then converts the byte stream to machine language which can then be read by any computer. Other platforms may or may not have this functionality.

Java is platform independent, which means that once the code is written, it can be run from anywhere. Most other platforms do not have this capability.

A Java programmer may develop Java code on any PC, while this functionality may not be available on other platforms.

141. Can we overload or override main method in Java?

Yes, we can overload or override main method in Java.

142. Which two method you need to implement for key Object in HashMap?

To use any object as Key in HashMap, it must implement equals() and hashcode() method in Java.

143. What is the volatile keyword? How and why would you use it?

In Java, each thread has its own stack, including its own copy of variables it can access. When the thread is created, it copies the value of all accessible variables into its own stack.
The volatile keyword basically says to the JVM "Warning, this variable may be modified in another Thread".

In all versions of Java, the volatile keyword guarantees global ordering on reads and writes to a variable. This implies that every thread accessing a volatile field will read the variable's current value instead of (potentially) using a cached value.

144. What are static initializers and when would you use them?

A static initializer gives you the opportunity to run code during the initial loading of a class and it guarantees that this code will only run once and will finish running before your class can be accessed in any way.

They are useful for performing initialization of complex static objects or to register a type with a static registry, as JDBC drivers do.

145. What are method references, and how are they useful?

Method references are a feature of Java 8. They are effectively a subset of lambda expressions, because if a lambda expression can be used, then it might be possible to use a method reference, but not always. They can only be used to call a singular method, which obviously reduces the possible places they can be used, unless your code is written to cater for them.

146. What are the different ways to concatenate strings? and which approach is most efficient?

Below are the different ways to concatenate strings.

Using Plus ("+") operator

Using a StringBuilder or StringBuffer class.

Using the concat() method

The efficiency depends on what you are concatenating and how you are concatenating it.

Concatenating constants: Plus operator is more efficient than the other two as the JVM optimizes constants.

Concatenating String variables: Any one of the three methods should do the job

Concatenating in a for/while
loop: StringBuilder or StringBuffer is the most efficient.

147. What are the four main concepts of OOP?

Encapsulation, Polymorphism, Inheritance and Abstraction are the 4 main concepts or pillars of an object-oriented programming.

148. Explain different ways of creating a thread?

In addition to the JVM created threads, application developers can create new threads in Java. Threads can be created in many ways.

1.Extending the java.lang.Thread class.

2.Implementing the Java.lang.Runnable Interface.

3.Implementing the java. util.concurrent.Callable interface with the java. util.concurrent.Executor framework to pool the threads.

149. What will happen if we put a key object in a HashMap which is already there?

If you put the same key again then it will replace the old mapping because HashMap doesn't allow duplicate keys. The Same key will result in the same hashcode and will end up at the same position in the bucket.

Each bucket contains a linked list of Map.Entry object, which contains both Key and Value. Now Java will take the Key object from each entry and compare with this new key using equals () method, if that return true then value object in that entry will be replaced by new value.

150. Difference between CountDownLatch and CyclicBarrier in Java

Both CyclicBarrier and CountDownLatch are used to implement a scenario where one Thread waits for one or more Thread to complete their job before starts processing but there is one Difference between CountDownLatch and CyclicBarrier in Java which separates them apart and that is, you cannot reuse same CountDownLatch instance once count reaches to zero and latch is open, on the other hand CyclicBarrier can be reused by resetting Barrier, once barrier is broken.

****

Interview Q & A in JSP

1.What is JSP?

Java Server Pages (JSP) is a technology for developing webpages that supports dynamic content. This helps developers insert java code in HTML pages by making use of special JSP tags, most of which start with <% and end with %>.

2. Is JSP technology extensible?

YES. JSP technology is extensible as it allows to create custom actions or tags for a large no. of use cases. JSTL libraries enable this functionality in a JSP page.

3. What is a JSP declarations?

JSP Declarations help to declare the class variables and methods in a JSP page. They get initialized along with the initialization of the class. Everything in a <declaration> is accessible to the whole JSP page. You can encircle a declaration block within the <%! And %> tags.

4. What is a JSP expression?

A JSP expression helps to write an output without using the <out. Print statement>. You can see it as a shorthand description for the scriptlets. And as usual, you delimit an expression using the <%= and %> tags.

5. Explain the benefits of JSP.

The following are the benefits of a Java Server Pages:

Provide a large range of API to increase the result-oriented functionality.

Easily deployable and performance is robust on multiple requests.

Memory management and exception management is optimized.

The features portability, reusability and logic components of java language can be utilized across the platforms.

6.What are the JSP standard actions?

The JSP standard actions affect the overall runtime behavior of a JSP page and the response sent back to the client.

They can be used to include a file at the request time, to find or instantiate a JavaBean, to forward a request to a new page, to generate a browser-specific code, etc.

7.What are the standard actions available in JSP?

The standard actions available in JSP are as follows:

<jsp:include>: It includes a response from a servlet or a JSP page into the current page. It differs from an include directive in that it includes a resource at request processing time, whereas the include directive includes a resource at translation time.

<jsp:forward>: It forwards a response from a servlet or a JSP page to another page.

<jsp:useBean>: It makes a JavaBean available to a page and instantiates the bean.

<jsp:setProperty>: It sets the properties for a JavaBean.

<jsp:getProperty>: It gets the value of a property from a JavaBean component and adds it to the response.

<jsp:param>: It is used in conjunction with <jsp:forward>; <jsp: or plugin>; to add a parameter to a request. These parameters are provided using the name-value pairs.

<jsp:plugin>: It is used to include a Java applet or a JavaBean in the current JSP page.

8. Compare between Servlet and JSP?

In servlets HTML is written inside java code using print statements. In JSP java code is embedded inside HTML.

JSP pages are converted to servlets by the web container so actually it can do the same thing as java servlets.

JSP are easier for creating HTML content but servlets are easier for writing the java code.

A combination of JSP and servlet can be used to separate the presentation(HTML) and logic (java code) and taking the advantage of both.

9. Explain JSP life cycle phases?

A JSP Lifecycle consists of following steps:

Compilation –

The compilation process involves three steps:

Parsing the JSP.

Turning the JSP into a servlet.

Compiling the servlet.

Initialization – When a container loads a JSP it invokes the jspInit() method before servicing any requests

Execution – Whenever a browser requests a JSP and the page has been loaded and initialized, the JSP engine invokes the _jspService() method in the JSP. The _jspService() method of a JSP is invoked once per a request and is responsible for generating the response for that request and this method is also responsible for generating responses to all seven of the HTTP methods i.e. GET, POST, DELETE etc.

Cleanup – The destruction phase of the JSP life cycle represents when a JSP is being removed from use by a container. The jspDestroy() method is the JSP equivalent of the destroy method for servlets.

10. What is the difference between HTML and JSP comments?

HTML comments are passed during the translation phase and hence can be viewed in the page source in the browser. JSP comments are converted to normal java comments during the translation process and will not appear in the output page source.

11. What are JSP implicit objects?

Implicit objects in JSP are the objects that are created by the web container automatically and the container makes them available to the JSP to access it. Implicit objects are available only inside the _jspService() method hence cannot be accessed anywhere outside.

12. List all the JSP implicit objects?

List of implicit objects are

request

response

session

application

page

pagecontext

out

config

exception.

13. What are the advantages of JSP over Active Server Pages (ASP)?

The advantages of JSP over ASP are

The dynamic part is written in Java, not in Visual Basic (VB) or other MS specific language, so it is more powerful and easier to use.

It is portable to other operating systems and non-Microsoft Web Servers.

14. What are the different scope values for the JSP action?

The scope attribute identifies the lifecycle of the Action element. It has four possible values: (a) page, (b)request, (c)session, and (d) application.

15. What is a request object?

The request object is an instance of a javax.servlet.http.HttpServletRequest object. Each time a client requests a page the JSP engine creates a new object to represent that request.

The request object provides methods to get HTTP header information including form data, cookies, HTTP methods etc.

16. What are JSP implicit objects?

JSP Implicit Objects are the Java objects that the JSP Container makes available to developers in each page and developer can call them directly without being explicitly declared. JSP Implicit Objects are also called pre-defined variables.

17. What is a response object?

The response object is an instance of a javax.servlet.http.HttpServletRequest object. Just as the server creates the request object, it also creates an object to represent the response to the client.

The response object also defines the interfaces that deal with creating new HTTP headers. Through this object the JSP programmer can add new cookies or date stamps, HTTP status codes etc.

18.What is the out implicit object?

The out implicit object is an instance of a javax.servlet.jsp.JspWriter object and is used to send content in a response.

19.What implicit objects are supported by JSP?

request, response, out, session, application, config, pageContext, page, Exception

20.What is an application Object?

The application object is direct wrapper around the ServletContext object for the generated Servlet and, an instance of a javax.servlet.ServletContext object.

This object is a representation of the JSP page through its entire lifecycle. This object is created when the JSP page is initialized and will be removed when the JSP page is removed by the jspDestroy() method.

21.What is a config Object?

The config object is an instantiation of javax.servlet.ServletConfig and is a direct wrapper around the ServletConfig object for the generated servlet.

This object allows the JSP programmer access to the Servlet or JSP engine initialization parameters such as the paths or file locations etc.

22.What is a pageContext Object?

The pageContext object is an instance of a javax.servlet.jsp.PageContext object. The pageContext object is used to represent the entire JSP page.

This object stores references to the request and response objects for each request. The application, config, session, and out objects are derived by accessing attributes of this object.

The pageContext object also contains information about the directives issued to the JSP page, including the buffering information, the errorPageURL, and page scope.

23.What is a page object?

This object is an actual reference to the instance of the page. It can be thought of as an object that represents the entire JSP page.

The page object is really a direct synonym for this object.

24.What is an exception Object?

The exception object is a wrapper containing the exception thrown from the previous page. It is typically used to generate an appropriate response to the error condition.

25.What is JSTL?

The Java Server Pages Standard Tag Library (JSTL) is a collection of useful JSP tags which encapsulates core functionality common to many JSP applications.

JSTL has support for common, structural tasks such as iteration and conditionals, tags for manipulating XML documents, internationalization tags, and SQL tags. It also provides a framework for integrating existing custom tags with JSTL tags.

26.What the different types of JSTL tags?

Types of JSTL tags are –

Core Tags

Formatting tags

SQL tags

XML tags

JSTL Functions

27. What do you understand of the JSP directives?

JSP directives are the instructions for the JSP container to control the processing of the whole page.

They add the ability to set global values such as a class declaration, method definition, output data type, etc.

They don't send any output to the client.

All directives should get enclosed within <%@ %> tag.

e.g. page and include directive, etc.

28. What do you understand of the page directive?

It notifies the JSP container of the headers (facilities) that the page receives from the environment.

Usually, the page directive remains at the top of a JSP page.

A JSP page can have any number of page directives if the attribute – value pair is unique.

The include directive syntax is: <%@ page attribute="value">

e.g.:<%@ include file="header.jsp" %>

29.Explain the different attributes of a page directive?

There are about 13-attributes available for a page directive. Some of the important ones are as follows:

<import>: Signifies the packages that get queued for import.

<session>: Specifies the session data available to the JSP page.

<contentType>: Allows a user to update the content-type for a page.

<isELIgnored>: Specifies if an EL expression gets ignored during the translation of the JSP to a servlet.

30.What is the include directive?

Its purpose is to attach the static resources to the current JSP page during the translation process. The include directive syntax is as follows:

<%@ include file = “File-Name” %>

The include directive statically embeds the contents of a resource into the current JSP.

It allows a user to reuse the code without duplicating it and inserts the data of the target file during JSP translation.

This directive has only one attribute called <file> that specifies the name of the file to include.

31. What are the different JSP scripting elements?

There are three types of scripting language elements:

Declarations,

Scriptlets, and

Expressions.

32.What is a buffer attribute?

The buffer attribute specifies buffering characteristics for the server output response object.

33.What happens when buffer is set to a value “none”?

When buffer is set to “none”, servlet output is immediately directed to the response output object.

34. What is isScriptingEnabled Attribute?

The isScriptingEnabled attribute determines if scripting elements are allowed for use.

The default value (true) enables scriptlets, expressions, and declarations. If the attribute's value is set to false, a translation-time error will be raised if the JSP uses any scriptlets, expressions (non-EL), or declarations.

35.What is autoFlush attribute?

The autoFlush attribute specifies whether buffered output should be flushed automatically when the buffer is filled, or whether an exception should be raised to indicate buffer overflow.

A value of true (default) indicates automatic buffer flushing and a value of false throws an exception.

36.What is contentType attribute?

The contentType attribute sets the character encoding for the JSP page and for the generated response page. The default content type is text/html, which is the standard content type for HTML pages.

37.What is errorPage attribute?

The errorPage attribute tells the JSP engine which page to display if there is an error while the current page runs. The value of the errorPage attribute is a relative URL.

38.What is isErrorPage attribute?

The isErrorPage attribute indicates that the current JSP can be used as the error page for another JSP.

The value of isErrorPage is either true or false. The default value of the isErrorPage attribute is false.

39.What is extends attribute?

The extends attribute specifies a superclass that the generated servlet must extend.

40.What is import attribute?

The import attribute serves the same function as, and behaves like, the Java import statement. The value for the import option is the name of the package you want to import.

41.What is info attribute?

The info attribute lets you provide a description of the JSP.

42.What is isThreadSafe attribute?

The isThreadSafe option marks a page as being thread-safe. By default, all JSPs are considered thread-safe. If you set the isThreadSafe option to false, the JSP engine makes sure that only one thread at a time is executing your JSP.

43.What is language attribute?

The language attribute indicates the programming language used in scripting the JSP page.

44.What is session attribute?

The session attribute indicates whether the JSP page uses HTTP sessions. A value of true means that the JSP page has access to a built-in session object and a value of false means that the JSP page cannot access the built-in session object.

45.What is isELIgnored Attribute?

The isELIgnored option gives you the ability to disable the evaluation of Expression Language (EL) expressions.

The default value of the attribute is true, meaning that expressions, ${...}, are evaluated as dictated by the JSP specification. If the attribute is set to false, then expressions are not evaluated but rather treated as static text.

46. What is JSP action tag?

JSP action tags are a set of predefined tags provided by the JSP container to perform some common tasks thus reducing the java code in JSP.

47. What is a custom tag?

Custom tags are nothing but tags which are developed by programmers for performing specific functionalities.

48. Why JSP custom tags are required?

Any common code which needs to be reused across the web application can be developed using custom tags. It is easy to maintain as the logic is centralized. Any change to the logic just requires a one place change thus reducing the effort to change it.

49. Explain the difference between jsp include and directive include?

When we need to include static resource during the translation time, the '<%@ include>' is used. The JSP include is used when we need to have dynamic or static data at run time.

50. What is required to run JSP? Do I need to install the J2EE SDK, or do I only need a web server?

Java Server Pages (JSP) require a web server and a Java 2 Platform, Standard Edition (J2SE) Implementation to run. The J2EE SDK, has the functionality needed for running JSP pages. JSP technology is one of the J2EE SDK technologies. If you want to use JSP pages with other J2EE SDK technologies, e.g. Enterprise JavaBean ("EJB") technology, using the J2EE SDK are a good choice.

51. What is the main difference between include action and include directive?

Unlike the include directive, which inserts the file at the time the JSP page is translated into a servlet, include action inserts the file at the time the page is requested.

52. What is the difference between JSPWriter and PrintWriter?

The JSPWriter object contains most of the same methods as the java.io.PrintWriter class. However, JSPWriter has some additional methods designed to deal with buffering. Unlike the PrintWriter object, JSPWriter throws IOExceptions.

53. What is difference between GET and POST method in HTTP protocol?

The GET method sends the encoded user information appended to the page request. The page and the encoded information are separated by the? Character.

The POST method packages the information in the same way as GET methods, but instead of sending it as a text string after a?

in the URL it sends it as a separate message. This message comes to the backend program in the form of the standard input which you can parse and use for your processing.

54. What are JSP actions?

JSP actions use constructs in XML syntax to control the behavior of the servlet engine. You can dynamically insert a file, reuse JavaBeans components, forward the user to another page, or generate HTML for the Java plugin.

55. What is a TLD file?

TLD stands for Tag Library Descriptor. TLD file is an XML file containing details of all the tags being created. It should be placed in web-inf directory.

56. Name JSP bean object scopes and explain them briefly?

Bean object scopes are:

page: It is available only within the JSP page and is destroyed when the page has finished generating its output for the request.

request: It is valid for the current request and is destroyed when the response is sent.

session: It is valid for a user session and is destroyed when the session is destroyed.

application: valid throughout the application and is destroyed when the web application is destroyed/uninstalled.

57. What is the use of jsp:forward action tag?

The forward action tag is used to transfer control to a static or dynamic resource. The forward action terminates the action of the current page and forwards the request to another resource such as a static page, another JSP page, or a java servlet. The static or dynamic resource to which control must be transferred is represented as a URL. The user can have the target file as a HTML file, another JSP file, or a servlet.

58. What is an expression language?

Expression language is a simple language for accessing data stored in java beans. This was introduced with the JSP 2.0 specification. It can also be used to access the values from implicit objects like page, context, header, cookie etc.

59. How expression language is specified?

Expression language is specified within curly braces and prefixed with a dollar sign.

Example: ${person.name}

Where 'person' is the java bean and 'name' is the java bean property.

60. What are the session management techniques in JSP?

The session management techniques used in servlets are also applicable to handle session in JSP also. The following are the techniques used to manage session in JSP:

URL rewriting

Hidden field

Cookie

Session object

61. What is a JSP directive?

A directive provides meta data information about the JSP file to the web container. Web container uses this during the translation/compilation phase of the JSP life cycle.

62.Give few examples of JSP directives?

Examples of JSP directive are:

Importing tag libraries

Import required classes

Set output buffering options

Include content from external files.

63. What are the different types of JSP directives?

The JSP specification defines three directives:

Page directive: Provides information about page, such as scripting language that is used, content type, or buffer size etc.

Include directive: Used to include the content of external files.

Taglib directive: Used to import custom tags defined in tag libraries. Custom tags are typically developed by developers.

64. What is the syntax for JSP directive?

A JSP directive is declared using following syntax:

<%@directive attribute="value" %>

Where, directive – The type of directive (page, taglib or include) attribute – Represents the behavior to be set for the directive to act upon.

65. What is page directive in JSP?

The page directive is used to provide the metadata about the JSP page to the container. Page directives may be coded anywhere in JSP page. By standards, page directives are coded at the top of JSP page. A page can have any number of page directives.

Syntax: <%@page attribute1="value" attribute2="value" %>

66. What is the work of include directive?

This directive inserts a HTML file, JSP file or text file at translation time. The include process is not dynamic, it means that the text of the included file is added to the JSP file like copy pasting the contents.

67. Does included file in include directive contain <html> or <body> tags and why?

Included file should not contain <html> or <body> tags because the entire content of the included file is added to the main JSP file, these tags would conflict with the same tags in the main JSP file, causing an error.

68. What is a scriptlet?

A scriptlet contains Java code that is executed every time a JSP is invoked. When a JSP is translated to a servlet, the scriptlet code goes into the service()method. Hence, methods and variables written in scriptlets are local to the service() method. A scriptlet is written between the <% and %> tags and is executed by the container at request processing time.

69. What are JSP declarations?

As the name implies, JSP declarations are used to declare class variables and methods in a JSP page. They are initialized when the class is initialized. Anything defined in a declaration is available for the whole JSP page. A declaration block is enclosed between the <%! and %> tags. A declaration is not included in the service() method when a JSP is translated to a servlet.

70. What is a JSP expression?

A JSP expression is used to write an output without using the out.print statement. It can be said as a shorthand representation for scriptlets. An expression is written between the <%= and %> tags. It is not required to end the expression with a semicolon, as it implicitly adds a semicolon to all the expressions within the expression tags.

71.How is scripting disabled?

Scripting is disabled by setting the scripting-invalid element of the deployment descriptor to true. It is a sub element of jsp-property-group. Its valid values are true and false. The syntax for disabling scripting is as follows:

```
<jsp-property-group>

<URL-pattern>*.jsp</URL-pattern>

<scripting-invalid>true</scripting-invalid>

</jsp-property-group>
```

72. What is the difference between include directive and include action?

Include directive:

The include directive, includes the content of the specified file during the translation phase–when the page is converted to a servlet.

The include directive is used to statically insert the contents of a resource into the current JSP.

Use the include directive if the file changes rarely. It's the fastest mechanism.

Include action:

The include action, includes the response generated by executing the specified page (a JSP page or a servlet) during the request processing phase–when the page is requested by a user.

The include standard action enables the current JSP page to include a static or a dynamic resource at runtime.

Use the include action only for content that changes often, and if which page to include cannot be decided until the main page is requested.

73. What is the best way to implement a thread-safe JSP page?

Apply the SingleThreadModel Interface in the JSP page.

You can get this done by adding the directive given in the below example.

<%@page isThreadSafe=" false" %>

74. Is it possible from a JSP page to process HTML form content?

Yes. You can fetch the data from the input elements of the form by using the request's implicit object. It lies either as a scriptlet or an expression. Next, there is no need to implement any HTTP methods like doGet() or doPost() in the JSP page.

75.What are the different scripting elements available in JSP?

JSP scripting elements let you embed the Java code into the servlet. Three forms of scripting elements are available in the JSP.

Expression syntax is <%= Expression %>. They get evaluated and inserted into the output.

Scriptlet syntax is <% Code %>. They get inserted into the servlet's service method.

A Declaration follows the syntax <%! Code %>. They get attached to the body of the servlet class, outside of any existing methods.

76.Which of the JSP life cycle methods you can override?

You can't override the _jspService() Method within a JSP page. However, there are two approaches you can take to override the jspInit() and jspDestroy() methods within the JSP page.

jspInit() Can be quite useful for reserving resources like DB connections, N/W connections, and so forth for the JSP page. It is deemed as a good programming practice to free any allocated resources in the jspDestroy() method.

77. What is the session Object?

The session object is an instance of javax.servlet.http.httpsession and is used to track client session between client requests

78.How to prevent the page errors from printing in a JSP page?

Setup an "ErrorPage" attribute of the PAGE directory to the name of the error page in the JSP page template. And then use the following setting in the error page JSP.

isErrorpage=" TRUE"

With the above attribute, you can stop the errors from getting displayed

79.What are the types of elements in JSP?

There are four types of elements in JSP:

Directives

Actions

Scripting

Comments

80.How variable behaves defined inside a scriptlet element and declaration element?

Variable defined inside scriptlet are like method local variables once the method execution is complete the value stored would be lost. Variables defined inside declaration are like class level instance variables and values will be retained across user requests.

81.What is a Tag Handler?

Tag handler is a java class that holds the logic of the custom tag.

82. How Tag handler is triggered?

Tag handler class is triggered by the web container whenever it encounters the custom tag in a JSP file.

83. Name the classes and interfaces which custom tag must implement or extend?

Custom tag must implement or extend any of the following interfaces or classes.

Tag interface

BodyTag interface

TagSupport class

BodyTagSupport class

SimpleTagSupport class

84. What is SimpleTagSupport class?

The SimpleTagSupport class is the base class intended to be used for developing tag handler. The SimpleTagSupport class implements the SimpleTag interface and defines API's which can be overridden by the custom tag handlers.

85.Explain the difference between ServletContext and PageContext?

The information about the container which the application is running is provided by the 'ServletContext'. The information about the Request in provided by the 'PageContext'

86.Explain the translation unit in a JSP?

JSP has the capability to include another HTML and JSP file in one JSP file. This feature is normally encompassed using the 'include' directive. When the JSP engine is presented with such a JSP page it is converted to one servlet class and this is called a translation unit, Things to remember in a translation unit is that page directives affect the whole unit, one variable declaration cannot occur in the same unit more than once, the standard action jsp:useBean cannot declare the same bean twice in one unit.

87. What is core tag?

Core tag specify several actions such as displaying content based on a condition, manipulating collections and managing URL's such as redirecting to a different page. It is used to do more common actions in easier and effective way whereby minimizing the use of scriptlets. It uses the prefix c.

88.How can you read a request header information?

Using getHeaderNames() method of HttpServletRequest to read the HTTP header information. This method returns an Enumeration that contains the header information associated with the current HTTP request.

89.How to read form data using JSP?

JSP handles form data parsing automatically using the following methods depending on the situation –

getParameter() – You call request.getParameter() method to get the value of a form parameter.

getParameterValues() – Call this method if the parameter appears more than once and returns multiple values, for example checkbox.

getParameterNames() – Call this method if you want a complete list of all parameters in the current request.

getInputStream() – Call this method to read binary data stream coming from the client.

90.What are filters?

JSP Filters are Java classes that can be used in JSP Programming for the following purposes –

To intercept requests from a client before they access a resource at back end.

To manipulate responses from server before they are sent back to the client.

91.How do you define filters?

Filters are defined in the deployment descriptor file web.xml and then mapped to either servlet or JSP names or URL patterns in your application's deployment descriptor.

When the JSP container starts up your web application, it creates an instance of each filter that you have declared in the deployment descriptor. The filters execute in the order that they are declared in the deployment descriptor.

92. What are cookies?

Cookies are text files stored on the client computer and they are kept for various information tracking purpose.

93. How to read cookies with JSP?

To read cookies, you need to create an array of javax.servlet.http.Cookie objects by calling the getCookies( ) method of HttpServletRequest. Then cycle through the array and use getName() and getValue() methods to access each cookie and associated value.

94. How to delete cookies with JSP?

To delete cookies is very simple. If you want to delete a cookie then you simply need to follow up following three steps –

Read an already existing cookie and store it in Cookie object.

Set cookie age as zero using setMaxAge() method to delete an existing cookie.

Add this cookie back into response header.

95. What is a hit count for a Webpage?

A hit counter tells you about the number of visits on a page of your web site.

96.How do you implement hit counter in JSP?

To implement a hit counter, you can make use of Application Implicit object and associated methods getAttribute() and setAttribute().

This object is a representation of the JSP page through its entire lifecycle. This object is created when the JSP page is initialized and will be removed when the JSP page is removed by the jspDestroy() method.

97.What is auto refresh feature?

Consider a webpage which is displaying live game score or stock market status or currency exchange ratio. For all such type of pages, you would need to refresh your Webpage regularly using refresh or reload button with your browser.

JSP makes this job easy by providing you a mechanism where you can make a webpage in such a way that it would refresh automatically after a given interval.

98.How do you implement the auto refresh in JSP?

The simplest way of refreshing a Webpage is using method setIntHeader() of response object. Following is the signature of this method –

public void setIntHeader(String header, int headerValue)

This method sends back header "Refresh" to the browser along with an integer value which indicates time interval in seconds.

99. What is Internationalization?

Internationalization means enabling a web site to provide different versions of content translated into the visitor's language or nationality.

100.What is Localization?

Localization is the process of adding resources to a web site to adapt it to a geographical or cultural region for example French translation to a web site.

****

Interview Q & A in EJB

1.What is EJB?

EJB stands for Enterprise Java Beans. EJB is a server-side software component that encapsulates business logic of an application. An EJB web container provides a runtime environment for web related software components, including computer security, Java servlet lifecycle management, transaction processing, and other web services.

2. What are the benefits of EJB?

Following are the key benefits of EJB.

Simplified development of large scale enterprise level application.

Application Server/ EJB container provides most of the system level services like transaction handling, logging, load balancing, persistence mechanism, exception handling and so on. Developer must focus only on business logic of the application.

EJB container manages life cycle of EJB instances thus developer needs not to worry about when to create/delete EJB objects.

3. What do you mean by EJB QL?

A query language which provides navigation through a network comprising enterprise beans and objects which are dependent and are defined by methods of container managed persistence. EJB 2.0 was the platform for introduction of EJB QL. It defines methods of finder which are used for entity beans, which has container managed persistence and has portability across persistence managers and containers. It is helpful in two kinds of finder methods: Finder methods, which have Home interface and return objects of entity. Select methods, which remain unexposed for the client to see but which the Bean provider uses.

4. How can one EJB be called from within another EJB?

An EJB can be called within another EJB by using JNDI which can be used for locating the Home Interface and acquiring the instance.

5. What are the implicit services provided by an EJB container?

Lifecycle Management:

Individual enterprise beans do not need to explicitly manage process allocation, thread management, object activation, or object destruction. The EJB container automatically manages the object lifecycle on behalf of the enterprise bean.

State Management:

Individual enterprise beans do not need to explicitly save or restore conversational object state between method calls. The EJB container automatically manages object state on behalf of the enterprise bean.

Security:

Individual enterprise beans do not need to explicitly authenticate users or check authorization levels. The EJB container automatically performs all security checking on behalf of the enterprise bean.

Transactions:

Individual enterprise beans do not need to explicitly specify transaction demarcation code to participate in distributed transactions. The EJB container can automatically manage the start, enrolment, commitment, and rollback of transactions on behalf of the enterprise bean.

Persistence:

Individual enterprise beans do not need to explicitly retrieve or store persistent object data from a database. The EJB container can automatically manage persistent data on behalf of the enterprise bean.

6. What are the different kinds of enterprise beans?

Stateless session bean- An instance of these non-persistent EJBs provides a service without storing an interaction or conversation state between methods. Any instance can be used for any client.

Stateful session bean- An instance of these non-persistent EJBs maintains state across methods and transactions. Each instance is associated with a client.

Entity bean- An instance of these persistent EJBs represents an object view of the data, usually rows in a database. They have a primary key as a unique identifier. Entity bean persistence can be either container-managed or bean-managed.

Message-driven bean- An instance of these EJBs is integrated with the Java Message Service (JMS) to provide the ability for message-driven beans to act as a standard JMS message consumer and perform asynchronous processing between the server and the JMS message producer.

7. What is bean managed transaction?

If a developer doesn't want a Container to manage transactions, it's possible to implement all database operations manually by writing the appropriate JDBC code. This often leads to productivity increase, but it makes an Entity Bean incompatible with some databases and it enlarges the amount of code to be written. All transaction management is explicitly performed by a developer.

8. What is advantage of putting business logic in EJB over stored procedure?

Putting complex business logic in stored procedure is not a good idea but it's been there for long time. Main advantage of using EJB over stored procedure is that you don't need to port your SQL Stored procedure code when you change database e.g. form Sybase to Oracle or Oracle to SQL Server.

9. Can we run EJB in web server like Tomcat?

No, you cannot run EJB in web server like Tomcat. You need application server like Glassfish, WebLogic or WebSphere to run Enterprise Java beans.

10. What is a transaction?

A transaction is a single unit of work items which follows the ACID properties. ACID stands for Atomic, Consistent, Isolated and Durable.

11. What is default interceptor in EJB?

Default interceptor is invoked for every bean within deployment. Default interceptor can be applied only via xml (ejb-jar.xml).

12. What is a timer service in EJB?

Timer Service is a mechanism using which scheduled application can be build. For example, salary slip generation on 1st of every month. EJB 3.0 specification has specified @Timeout annotation which helps in programming the ejb service in a stateless or message driven bean. EJB Container calls the method which is annotated by @Timeout.

13. Explain exception handling in EJB?

EJB has two types of exceptions:

System Exception: is an unchecked exception derived from java.lang.RuntimeException. A System Exception is thrown by the system and is not recoverable. For example, EJB container losing connection to the database server, failed remote method objects call etc. Because the System Exceptions are unpredictable, the EJB container is the only one responsible for trapping the System Exceptions. The container automatically wraps any Runtime Exception in RemoteException, which subsequently gets thrown to the caller (i.e. client). In addition to intercepting System Exception the container may log the errors.

Application Exception: is specific to an application and thrown because of violation of business rules (e.g. InsufficierntFundException etc.). An Application Exception is a checked exception that is either defined by the bean developer and does not extend java.rmi.RemoteException or is predefined in the javax.ejb package (i.e. CreateException, RemoveException, ObjectNotFoundException etc.). An Application Exception is specific to an application and is thrown because of violation of business rules. The client should be able to determine how to handle an Application Exception. If the account balance is zero, then an Application Exception like InsufficientFundException can be thrown. If an Application Exception should be treated as a System Exception then it needs to be wrapped in an EJBException, which extends java.lang.RuntimeException so that it can be managed properly (e.g. rolling back transactions) and propagated to the client.

14. Is Message Driven bean a stateless bean?

Message driven bean is a stateless bean and is used to do task asynchronously.

15. What a remote session bean is used in EJB?

if EJB client is in different environment where EJB session bean is to be deployed then we use remote session bean.

16. What is System Level Exception in EJB?

Any exception which is not caused by business logic or business code. RuntimeException, RemoteException are SystemException. For example, error during EJB lookup. Then EJB container treats such exception as System level exception.

17. What do you mean by re-entrant? Can you say that session beans as re-entrant? Can entity beans be specified as re-entrant?

If the entity bean is defined as re-entrant, then it is possible by multiple clients to associate with the Entity bean and get methods executed concurrently inside the entity bean. Synchronization is taken care of by container. There is an exception thrown when an entity beam is defined as non-re-entrant and numerous clients are connected to it concurrently to carry out a method.

18.Differentiate Conversational from Non-conversational interactions?

The interaction between the client and the bean is called conversational while where multi method conversations are not held with clients it is known as non-conversational interactions.

19. Can EJB made to handle multiple transactions?

EJB can be made to handle multiple transactions by enabling multiple Entity beans to handle every database and one Session Bean to retain transaction with the Entity Bean.

20. What is J2EE?

J2EE (Java 2 Enterprise Edition) is an environment for developing and deploying enterprise applications. The J2EE platform consists of J2EE components, services, Application Programming Interfaces (APIs) and protocols that provide the functionality for developing multi-tiered and distributed Web based applications.

21. Which is more beneficial: Stateful or Stateless Bean?

If a conversational state is needed then, Stateful mode is preferred while Stateless paradigm is preferred for a single business process.

22. Differentiate Phantom from Un-repeatable?

When data that did not existed before is inserted, it is read as phantom whereas when data that already existed is changed, un-repeatable occurs.

23. What do you mean by in-memory replication?

When the contents having the memory of a single physical m/c are simulated in all m/c in that cluster, that process is called memory replication.

24. What is Stateless Session Bean in EJB?

A stateless session bean is a type of enterprise bean which is normally used to do independent operations. A stateless session bean as per its name does not have any associated client state, but it may preserve its instance state. EJB Container normally creates a pool of few stateless bean's objects and use these objects to process client's request. Because of pool, instance variable values are not guaranteed to be same across lookups/method calls.

25. What is Message Driven Bean in EJB?

A message driven bean is a type of enterprise bean which is invoked by EJB container when it receives a message from queue or topic. Message driven bean is a stateless bean and is used to do task asynchronously.

26. What are the key components of persistence API in EJB?

Following are the key components of persistence API in EJB:

Entity - A persistent object representing the data-store record. It is good to be serializable.

Entity Manager - Persistence interface to do data operations like add/delete/update/find on persistent object(entity). It also helps to execute queries using Query interface.

Persistence unit (persistence.xml) - Persistence unit describes the properties of persistence mechanism.

Data Source (*ds.xml) - Data Source describes the data-store related properties like connection URL. user-name, password etc.

27. What is Callback in EJB?

Callback is a mechanism by which life cycle of an enterprise bean can be intercepted. EJB 3.0 specification has specified callbacks for which callback handler methods are to be created. EJB Container calls these callbacks. We can define callback methods in the ejb class itself or in a separate class. EJB 3.0 has provided many annotations for callbacks.

28. What is an EJB Interceptor?

EJB 3.0 provides specification to intercept business methods calls using methods annotated with @AroundInvoke annotation. An interceptor method is called by EJBContainer before business method call it is intercepting.

29. What is JNDI? Explain its terms in terms of EJB.

JNDI stands for Java Naming and Directory Interface. It is a set of API and service interfaces. Java based applications use JNDI for naming and directory services. In context of EJB, there are two terms:

Binding - This refers to assigning a name to an EJB object which can be used later.

Lookup - This refers to looking up and getting an object of EJB.

30. Define EAR, WAR and JAR?

JAR files contain all EJB classes.

WAR files contain all servlets, web component pages, gif, html, beans, applets, classes and classes.

EAR files contain both JAR and WAR files.

31. What do you mean by in-memory replication?

When the contents having the memory of a single physical m/c are simulated in all m/c in that cluster, that process is called memory replication.

32. Differentiate, "find a method" from "select method" in EJB?

A persistent field is returned by the select method of an entity bean that is related. A remote or local interface is returned by the finder method.

33. Define ejb Create () and EjbPostCreate ()?

When the method is called before the persistence storage is written with the bean state, it is ejbCreate ().

When the method is called after the persistence storage is written with the bean state, it is ejbPostCreate ().

34. Define Ripple Effect?

During runtime, when the changes made in the various properties of server group, are propagated in every associated clone, this process is known as Ripple Effect.

35. What are transactional attributes?

EJB transactions are a set of mechanisms and concepts, which insures the integrity and consistency of the database when multiple clients try to read/update the database simultaneously. Transaction attributes are defined at different levels like EJB class, a method within a class or segment of a code within a method. The attributes specified for a method take precedence over the attributes specified for a EJB class. Transaction attributes are specified declaratively through EJB deployment descriptors. Unless there is any compelling reason, the declarative approach is recommended over programmatic approach where all the transactions are handled programmatically. With the declarative approach, the EJB container will handle the transactions.

36. What are the different kinds of enterprise beans?

Session Bean:

It is a non-persistent object that implements some business logic running on the server. Session beans do not survive system shut down. There are two types of session beans

Stateless session beans (i.e. each session bean can be reused by multiple EJB clients).

Stateful session beans (i.e. each session bean is associated with one EJB client).

Entity Bean:

It is a persistent object that represents object views of the data, usually a row in a database. They have the primary key as a unique identifier. Multiple EJB clients can share each entity bean. Entity beans can survive system shutdowns. Entity beans can have two types of persistence

Container-Managed Persistence (CMP) - The container is responsible for saving the bean's state.

Bean-Managed Persistence (BMP): The entity bean is responsible for saving its own state.

Message-driven Bean:

It is integrated with the Java Message Service (JMS) to provide the ability to act as a message consumer and perform asynchronous processing between the server and the message producer.

37. What is EJB important in perspective of Java?

Enterprise JavaBeans (EJB) is a technology used on the server-side. It has a component architecture that is very essential for the maintenance and the developing a Java Platform. This is the technology that allows development of distributed, transactional, secure and portable applications made using the Java language. It allows modular approach to be taken to implement the enterprise level applications using the APIs that is provided with the technology itself. It provides a back end that allows easy writing of the business code for the enterprise applications. This provides the solutions for the problems to implement integrity, persistence and security. It gives transaction processing, concurrency control and other services like security, remote procedure call, etc.

38. What is class level interceptor in EJB?

Class level interceptor is invoked for every method of the bean. Class level interceptor can be applied both by annotation or via xml(ejb-jar.xml).

39.What is method level interceptor in EJB?

Method level interceptor is invoked for a method of the bean. Method level interceptor can be applied both by annotation of via xml(ejb-jar.xml).

40. What is the difference between a component and a service?

A component is an application level software unit as shown in the table above. All the J2EE components depend on the container for the system level support like transactions, security, pooling, life cycle management, threading etc. A service is a component that can be used remotely through a remote interface either synchronously or asynchronously (e.g. Web service, messaging system, sockets, RPC etc.). A service is a step up from "distributed objects". A service is a function that has a clearly defined service contract (e.g. interface, XML contract) to their consumers or clients, self-contained and does not depend on the context or state of other services.

41. List out the Declarative Transaction types.

They are:

mandatory

required

requires_new

supports

not_supported

never

42. Differentiate Conversational from Non-conversational interactions?

The interaction between the client and the bean is called conversational while where multi method conversations are not held with clients it is known as non-conversational interactions.

43. What is the difference between a Web server and an application server?

A Web server can be either a computer program or a computer running a program that is responsible for accepting HTTP requests from clients, serving back HTTP responses along with optional data contents, which usually are web pages such as HTML documents and linked objects on it. An application server is the kind of software engine that will deliver various applications to another device. It is the kind of computer found in an office or college network that allows everyone in the network to run software off the same machine.

44. How is consistency maintained by Stateful Session through transaction updates?

The data consistency is maintained by updating their fields every time a commitment of the transaction is made.

45. Define ACID Properties?

ACID is Atomicity, Consistency, Isolation and Durability.

Atomicity: Operations that are bundled together and projected a single unit of job.

Consistency: Guarantees that after a transaction has taken place, there will be consistency.

Isolation: Helps protect viewing of other simultaneous incomplete transaction results.

Durability: Ensures durability by keeping a transitional log by which the permanent data be recreated by again applying the steps involved.

46. How does EJB invocation take place?

Home Object reference is retrieved from the Naming Service via JNDI. Home Object reference is returned to the client. The steps are:

Created a new EJB Object via Home Object interface.

Created an EJB Object from the Ejb Object.

Returned an EJB Object reference to the client.

Invoked business method by using EJB Object reference.

Delegate requested to Bean (Enterprise Bean).

47. What are transaction isolation levels in EJB?

Transaction_read_uncommitted- Allows a method to read uncommitted data from a DB (fast but not wise).

Transaction_read_committed- Guarantees that the data you are getting has been committed.

Transaction_repeatable_read - Guarantees that all reads of the database will be the same during the transaction (good for read and update operations).

Transaction_serializable- All the transactions for resource are performed serial.

48. Difference between CMP and BMP.

CMP (Container Managed Persistence) developer does not have to write any data logic, the container manages the persistence of the entity bean. A CMP bean developer doesn't need to worry about JDBC code and transactions, because the Container performs database calls and transaction management instead of the programmer.

BMP (Bean-managed persistence) manages the synchronization of its state and the database that is directed by the container. It uses the database API that can read and write the fields present in the database. The synchronization operation can be performed to manage the transactions automatically for the bean. BMP allows full flexibility to be given to the developer for persistence operations that are complicated for the container and doesn't have the supported data source.

49. Which one is more beneficial: CMP or BMP?

When "one to one" mapping is involved, and the data is stored persistently is regional database, CMP is preferred. But when no "one to one" mapping is there, and data is retrieved from numerous tables having a complex query, Bean Managed Persistence is used.

50. Explain annotation in EJB to do the database entity relationships/mappings.

EJB 3.0 provides option to define database entity relationships/mappings like one to one, one to many, many to one and many to many relationships. Following are the relevant annotations:

OneToOne - Objects are having one to one relationship. For example, a passenger can travel using a single ticket at time.

OneToMany - Objects are having one to many relationships. For example, a father can have multiple kids.

ManyToOne - Objects are having many to one relationship. For examples, multiple kids having a single mother.

ManyToMany - Objects are having many to many relationships. For examples, a book can have multiple authors and an author can write multiple books.

51. What are the attributes of Bean Managed Transactions?

In Bean Managed Transactions, Transactions can be managed by handling exceptions at application level. Following are the key points to be considered:

Start - When to start a transaction in a business method.

Success - Identify success scenario when a transaction is to be committed.

Failed - Identify failure scenario when a transaction is to be rollback.

52. Can remove () be a Stateless Session bean?

Yes, remove () can be a Stateless Session bean because the life remains the same till the method is executed.

53. What is the difference between stateful and stateless session beans?

Stateless Session Beans

Do not have an internal state. Can be reused by different clients.

Need not be activated or passivated since the beans are pooled and reused.

Stateful Session Bean

Do have an internal state. Reused by the same client.

Need to handle activation and passivation to conserve system memory since one session bean object per client.

54. Can an EJB client invoke a method on a bean directly?

An EJB client should never access an EJB directly. Any access is done through the container. The container will intercept the client call and apply services like transaction, security etc. prior to invoking the actual EJB.

56. How to rollback a container managed transaction in EJB?

The way the exceptions are handled affects the way the transactions are managed. When the container manages the transaction, it is automatically rolled back when a System Exception occurs. This is possible because the container can intercept System Exception. However, when an Application Exception occurs, the container does not intercept it and therefore leaves it to the code to roll back using ctx.setRollbackOnly().

Be aware that handling exceptions in EJB is different from handling exceptions in Java. The Exception handling best practice tips are:

If you cannot recover from System Exception let the container handle it.

If a business rule is violated, then throw an application exception.

If you want to rollback a transaction on an application exception, then catch the application exception and throw an EJBException or use ctx.setRollbackOnly();

57. What is the difference between session and entity beans?

Session Beans:

Session Beans represent a process or flow.

Each session bean is associated with one EJB client at a time.

Session Beans are thread safe.

Session beans are used for application logic.

Session beans control the workflow and transactions of a group of entity beans.

Do not survive when system shut downs or server crashes.

Entity Beans:

Entity bean represent row in a database.

Use entity beans to develop persistent object model.

Each entity bean is associated with more than one client at a time.

Do survive when system shut downs or server crashes.

Entity beans are persistent.

58.What is Lazy loading?

Lazy loading is a design pattern commonly used in computer programming to defer initialization of an object until the point at which it is needed. It can contribute to efficiency in the program's operation if properly and appropriately used.

59. What is the difference between JavaBeans and enterprise java beans?

JavaBean is simply a class that subclasses java.awt.Component and implements object serialization or externalization. It is low-level approach to developer reusable software components that can be used for building different types of Java applications (applets, stand-alone apps,) in any area. Whether you're developing a simple applet or a complicated application, JavaBeans can be integrated into your system with ease. Whereas EJB An Enterprise JavaBean - an EJB - is a reusable server-side software component. EJB facilitate the development of distributed Java applications, providing an object-oriented transactional environment for building distributed, multitier enterprise components. An EJB is a remote object, which needs the services of an EJB container in which to execute.

****

Interview Q & A in Servlet

1.What is a Servlet?

Servlet can be described in many ways, depending on the context.

Servlet is a technology i.e. used to create web application.

Servlet is an API that provides many interfaces and classes including documentations.

Servlet is an interface that must be implemented for creating any servlet.

Servlet is a class that extend the capabilities of the servers and respond to the incoming request. It can respond to any type of requests.

Servlet is a web component that is deployed on the server to create dynamic web page.

2. Explain servlet life cycle.

A servlet life cycle can be defined as the entire process from its creation till the destruction. The following are the paths followed by a servlet.

Servlet Life Cycle consists of three methods:

public void init(ServletConfig config) – This method is used by container to initialize the servlet, this method is invoked only once in the lifecycle of servlet.

public void service(ServletRequest request, ServletResponse response) – This method is called once for every request, container can't invoke service() method until unless init() method is executed.

public void destroy() – This method is invoked once when servlet is unloaded from memory.

3. What is different between web server and application server?

A web server responsibility is to handler HTTP requests from client browsers and respond with HTML response. A web server understands HTTP language and runs on HTTP protocol.
Apache Web Server is kind of a web server and then we have specific containers that can execute servlets and JSPs known as servlet container, for example Tomcat.
Application Servers provide additional features such as Enterprise JavaBeans support, JMS Messaging support, Transaction Management etc. So, we can say that Application server is a web server with additional functionalities to help developers with enterprise applications.

4. What is HTTPServletRequest class?

When a browser requests for a web page, it sends lot of information to the web server which cannot be read directly because this information travel as a part of header of HTTP request. HTTPServletRequest represents this HTTP Request.

5.What is HTTPServletResponse class?

When a Web server responds to a HTTP request to the browser, the response typically consists of a status line, some response headers, a blank line, and the document. HTTPServletResponse represents this HTTP Response.

6. What are the advantages of servlets over CGI?

Servlets offer several advantages in comparison with the CGI.

Performance is significantly better.

Servlets execute within the address space of a Web server. It is not necessary to create a separate process to handle each client request.

Servlets are platform-independent because they are written in Java.

Java security manager on the server enforces a set of restrictions to protect the resources on a server machine. So, servlets are trusted.

The full functionality of the Java class libraries is available to a servlet. It can communicate with applets, databases, or other software via the sockets and RMI mechanisms that you have seen already.

7. How to get the IP address of client in servlet?

We can use request.getRemoteAddr() to get the client IP address in servlet.

8. How to get the server information in a servlet?

We can use below code snippet to get the servlet information in a servlet through servlet context object.

getServletContext().getServerInfo()

9. What is URL Encoding?

URL Encoding is the process of converting data into CGI form so that it can travel across the network without any issues. URL Encoding strip the white spaces and replace special characters with escape characters. We can use java.net.URLEncoder.encode(String str, String unicode) to encode a String. URL Decoding is the reverse process of encoding and we can use java.net.URLDecoder.decode(String str, String unicode) to decode the encoded string.

10. What is difference between ServletConfig and ServletContext?

Some of the differences between ServletConfig and ServletContext are:

ServletConfig is a unique object per servlet whereas ServletContext is a unique object for complete application.

ServletConfig is used to provide init parameters to the servlet whereas ServletContext is used to provide application level init parameters that all other servlets can use.

We can't set attributes in ServletConfig object whereas we can set attributes in ServletContext that other servlets can use in their implementation.

11. Explain what is a session?

The session is an object used by a servlet to track a user's interaction with a Web application across multiple HTTP requests. The session is stored on the server.

12.What is the use of ServletContext ?

Using ServletContext, we can access data from its environment. Servlet context is common to all Servlets, so all Servlets share the information through ServeltContext.

13. How can we create a Servlet?

A Servlet can be created by extending the httpServlet or GenericServlet classes.

14. What do you mean by lazy loading of a Servlet?

A container does not initialize the servlets as soon as it starts up, it initializes a servlet when it receives a request for that servlet first time. This is called lazy loading.

15. What do you mean by pre-initialization of a Servlet?

The process of loading a servlet before any request comes in is called preloading or pre-initializing a Servlet.

16. What is ServletConfig object?

javax.servlet.ServletConfig is used to pass configuration information to Servlet. Every servlet has its own ServletConfig object and servlet container is responsible for instantiating this object. We can provide servlet init parameters in web.xml file or through use of WebInitParam annotation. We can use getServletConfig() method to get the ServletConfig object of the servlet.

17. What is ServletContext object?

javax.servlet.ServletContext interface provides access to web application parameters to the servlet. The ServletContext is unique object and available to all the servlets in the web application. When we want some init parameters to be available to multiple or all the servlets in the web application, we can use ServletContext object and define parameters in web.xml using <context-param> element. We can get the ServletContext object via the getServletContext() method of ServletConfig. Servlet containers may also provide context objects that are unique to a group of servlets and which is tied to a specific portion of the URL path namespace of the host.

18. What is the inter-servlet communication?

When we want to invoke another servlet from a servlet service method, we use inter-servlet communication mechanisms. We can invoke another servlet using RequestDispatcher forward() and include() methods and provide additional attributes in request for other servlet use.

19. What is servlet attributes and their scope?

Servlet attributes are used for inter-servlet communication, we can set, get and remove attributes in web application. There are three scopes for servlet attributes – request scope, session scope and application scope.

ServletRequest, HttpSession and ServletContext interfaces provide methods to get/set/remove attributes from request, session and application scope respectively.

Servlet attributes are different from init parameters defined in web.xml for ServletConfig or ServletContext.

20. What are servlet filters?

Servlet Filters are pluggable java components that we can use to intercept and process requests before they are sent to servlets and response after servlet code is finished and before container sends the response back to the client.

21.How servlet filters work?

Some common tasks that we can do with filters are:

Logging request parameters to log files.

Authentication and authorization of request for resources.

Formatting of request body or header before sending it to servlet.

Compressing the response data sent to the client.

Alter response by adding some cookies, header information etc.

22. What is the difference between using getSession(true) and getSession(false) methods?

getSession(true) – This method will check whether already a session is existing for the user. If a session is existing, it will return that session object, otherwise it will create new session

object and return that object.
getSession(false) – This method will check existence of session. If session exists, then it returns the reference of that session object, if not, this method will return null.

23. What is servlet mapping?

The servlet mapping defines an association between a URL pattern and a servlet. The mapping is used to map requests to Servlets.

24. How can we create deadlock situation in servlet?

We can create deadlock in servlet by making a loop of method invocation, just call doPost() method from doGet() method and doGet() method to doPost() method to create deadlock situation in servlet.

25. What is difference between GenericServlet and HttpServlet?

GenericServlet is protocol independent implementation of Servlet interface whereas HttpServlet is HTTP protocol specific implementation. Most of the times we use servlet for creating web application and that's why we extend HttpServlet class. HttpServlet class extends GenericServlet and provide some other methods specific to HTTP protocol.

26.What is cookies?

Cookies are text data sent by server to the client and it gets saved at the client local machine.

27. How does Cookies work in Servlets?

Servlet API provides cookies support through javax.servlet.http.Cookie class that implements Serializable and Cloneable interfaces.

HttpServletRequest getCookies() method is provided to get the array of Cookies from request, since there is no point of adding Cookie to request, there are no methods to set or add cookie to request.

Similarly, HttpServletResponse addCookie(Cookie c) method is provided to attach cookie in response header, there are no getter methods for cookie.

28. What is a deployment descriptor?

Deployment descriptor is a configuration file for the web application and its name is web.xml and it resides in WEB-INF directory. Servlet container use this file to configure web application servlets, servlet config params, context init params, filters, listeners, welcome pages and error handlers.

29. How service() method works in a servlet?

The service() method is the main method to perform the actual task. The servlet container (i.e. web server) calls the service() method to handle requests coming from the client(browsers) and to write the formatted response back to the client.

Each time the server receives a request for a servlet, the server spawns a new thread and calls service. The service() method checks the HTTP request type (GET, POST, PUT, DELETE, etc.) and calls doGet, doPost, doPut, doDelete, etc. methods as appropriate.

30. How to do servlet filter mapping?

Filters are deployed in the deployment descriptor file web.xml and then map to either servlet names or URL patterns in your application's deployment descriptor.

31. How to configure a central error handling page in servlets?

Use the error-page element in web.xml to specify the invocation of servlets in response to certain exceptions or HTTP status codes.

32. How to set session timeout in servlet?

setMaxInactiveInterval(int interval) of HTTPSession object specifies the time, in seconds, between client requests before the servlet container will invalidate this session.

33. How to delete a cookie using servlet?

Read an already existing cookie and store it in Cookie object.

Set cookie age as zero using setMaxAge() method to delete an existing cookie.

Add this cookie back into response header.

34. Explain the difference between HttpServlet and GenericServlet?

A GenericServlet has a service() method to handle the requests. HttpServlet extends GenericServlet and adds support for doGet (), doPost () methods doPut (), doOptions (), doDelete (), doTrace () methods.

35. What is MIME Type?

The “Content-Type” response header is known as MIME Type. Server sends MIME type to client to let them know the kind of data it’s sending. It helps client in rendering the data for user. Some of the mostly used mime types are text/html, text/xml, application/xml etc.

We can use ServletContext getMimeType() method to get the correct MIME type of the file and use it to set the response content type. It’s very useful in downloading file through servlet from server.

36. How to detect locale in Servlets?

Following is the method of request object which returns Locale object.

java.util.Locale request.getLocale()

37.How to get country name in Servlets?

Following method returns a name for the locale's country that is appropriate for display to the user.

String getDisplayCountry()

38. How to set auto page refresh in servlet?

The simplest way of refreshing a web page is using method setIntHeader() of response object.

39. What is session?

Session provides a way to identify a user across more than one-page request or visit to a Web site and to store information about that user. The session persists for a specified time, across more than one connection or page request from the user.

40. How to redirect a request from a servlet to another servlet?

Page redirection is generally used when a document moves to a new location and we need to send the client to this new location or may be because of load balancing, or for simple randomization. The simplest way of redirecting a request to another page is using method sendRedirect() of response object.

41. How to read form data in servlet?

Servlets handles form data parsing automatically using the following methods depending on the situation:

getParameter(): You call request.getParameter() method to get the value of a form parameter.

getParameterValues(): Call this method if the parameter appears more than once and returns multiple values, for example checkbox.

getParameterNames(): Call this method if you want a complete list of all parameters in the current request.

42. When doGet() method of servlet to be called?

A GET request results from a normal request for a URL or from an HTML form that has no METHOD specified and it should be handled by doGet() method.

43. When doPost() method of servlet to be called?

A POST request results from an HTML form that specifically lists POST as the METHOD and it should be handled by doPost() method.

44. How to get the actual path of servlet in server?

We can use following code snippet to get the actual path of the servlet in file system.

getServletContext().getRealPath(request.getServletPath())

45. How to notify an object in session when session is invalidated or timed-out?

If we must make sure an object gets notified when session is destroyed, the object should implement javax.servlet.http.HttpSessionBindingListener interfa ce. This interface defines two callback methods – valueBound() and valueUnbound() that we can define to implement processing logic when the object is added as attribute to the session and when session is destroyed.

46. How do we call one servlet from another servlet?

We can use RequestDispatcher forward() method to forward the processing of a request to another servlet. If we want to include another servlet output to the response, we can use RequestDispatcher include() method.

47. Explain the difference between Authentication and authorization?

Authentication is the process where the application identifies who you are. Like user name and password.

Authorization, on the other hand, is when the application checks whether you're allowed to do that task. For instance, are you allowed to do delete or modify a resource. Application and thus can be used to share data between servlets.

48. What's the difference between servlets and applets?

Servlets executes on Servers. Applets executes on browser. Unlike applets, however, servlets have no graphical user interface.

49. Explain the difference between using getSession(false) and getSession(true) methods?

getSession(true) – This method will check whether already a session is existing for the user. If a session is existing, it will return that session object, otherwise it will create new session object and return that object.

getSession(false) – This method will check existence of session. If session exists, then it returns the reference of that session object, if not, this method will return null.

50. What is the use of servlet wrapper classes?

Servlet HTTP API provides two wrapper classes – HttpServletRequestWrapper and HttpServletResponseWrapper. These wrapper classes are provided to help developers with custom implementation of servlet request and response types. We can extend these classes and override only specific methods we need to implement for custom request and response objects. These classes are not used in normal servlet programming.

****
****

Interview Q & A in JMS

1.What is JMS?

Java Message Service (JMS)is an API which allows the J2EE application component to create, send, read and receive messages.

2. What is Messaging?

Messaging is a method of communication between software components and applications. A messaging system is a peer-to-peer facility: A messaging client can send messages to, and receive messages from, any other client. Each client connects to a messaging agent that provides services for creating, sending, receiving, and reading messages.

3. What are the type messaging provided by JMS?

There are two kinds of Messaging:

Synchronous

Asynchronous

4. What do you mean by Synchronous and Asynchronous type of messaging?

Synchronous: In this type of messaging, client waits for the server to respond to a message. Ex: Telephone call, two-way radio communication etc.

Asynchronous: In this type of messaging, client does not wait for a message from the server, but automatically an event is created to trigger a message from a server. Ex: email, text messaging, blog posting etc.

5. How may messaging models do JMS provide?

JMS provides for two messaging models,

1.publish-and-subscribe (pub/sub model)

2.point-to-point queuing. (P2P model)

6. What is the point-to-point model in JMS?

In P2P Model, a JMS Sender creates and sends messages to a Queue. Then a JMS Receiver or JMS Consumer receives and reads messages from a Queue. In P2P model, several receivers can exist, attached to the same queue. However, (Message Oriented Middleware) MOM will deliver the message to one and only one receiver.

7. What is JMS producer?

A JMS client that creates and sends messages.

8.What is JMS consumer?

JMS client that receives messages.

9.What is JMS message?

An object that contains the data being transferred between JMS clients.

10. Wat is JMS client?

An application or process that produces and/or receives messages.

11. Can we send e-mail messages using JMS?

JMS has no inherent support for email operations.

12. What are the types of messages that are supported by JMS?

The types of messages that are supported by JMS are

Stream Messages

Text Messages

Map Messages

Bytes Messages

Object Messages

13. What is Byte Message?

Byte message is a stream of uninterrupted bytes. It contains an array of primitive bytes in its payload. For the transfer of data between two applications in their native format, byte message is used, which may be not possible with other message types.

14. What is the important part of JMS applications?

Session

Connection

Message

Message Producer

Message Consumer

Connection factory and destination

15. Explain the difference between topic and queue?

Queue technique is used for one to one messaging, and it supports point to point messaging. While topic is typically used for one to many messaging and it supports public subscribe model of messaging.

16. What is the publish-and-subscribe model in JMS?

A publish-subscribe model is based on the message topic concept: Publishers send messages in a topic, and all subscribers of the given topic receive these messages.

17.What is publish/subscribe messaging?

The JMS publish/subscribe (Pub-Sub) message model is a one-to-many model. A publisher sends a message to a topic and all active subscribers of the topic receive the message. Subscribers that are not actively listening to the topic will miss the published message.

18.What is MOM about JMS?

The MOM (Message Oriented Middleware) is a software that works as an intermediate between two communicating components. It is placed between the client and server, MOM provides the facility of passing message by using the technique queuing. Until the client does not request to read the message, the messages will be stored in queue. By using this technique, the software component can work independently of time.

19. What is the main parts of JMS applications?

The main parts of JMS applications are:

Connection Factory and Destination

Connection

Session

Message Producer

Message Consumer

Message

20. What is the difference between Java Mail and JMS Queue?

JMS is the ideal high-performance messaging platform for intra business messaging, with full programmatic control over quality of service and delivery options.
Java Mail provides slow and human-readable messaging using infrastructure already available on virtually every computing platform.

21. What is the Role of the JMS Provider?

The JMS provider handles security of the messages, data conversion and the client triggering. The JMS provider specifies the level of encryption and the security level of the message, the best data type for the non-JMS client.

22. What is the difference between topic and queue?
A topic is typically used for one to many messaging i.e. it supports publish subscribe model of messaging. While queue is used for one-to-one messaging i.e. it supports Point to Point Messaging.

23. What are the advantages of JMS?

Asynchronous communications: An application need to notify another that an event has occurred with no need to wait for a response.

Reliability. Ensure once-and-only-once message delivery. With your DB approach you must "reinvent the wheel", especially if you have several clients reading the messages.

Loose coupling. Not all systems can communicate using a database. So JMS is pretty good to be used in heterogeneous environments with decoupled systems that can communicate over system boundaries.

24. How the JMS is different from RPC?

In RPC the method invoker waits for the method to finish execution and return the control back to the invoker. Thus, it is completely synchronous in nature. While in JMS the message sender just sends the message to the destination and continues its own processing. The sender does not wait for the receiver to respond. This is asynchronous behavior.

25. What is the basic difference between Publish Subscribe model and P2P model?

Publish Subscribe model is typically used in one-to-many situation. It is unreliable but very fast. P2P model is used in one-to-one situation. It is highly reliable.

26. What is the difference between Message producer and Message consumer?

Messaging systems provide a host of powerful advantages over other conventional distributed computing models. Primarily, they encourage "loose coupling" between message consumers and message producers. There is a high degree of anonymity between producer and consumer: to the message consumer, it doesn't matter who produced the message, where the producer lives on the network, or when the message was produced.

27. What is JMS session?

A JMS session is a single-threaded context for sending and receiving JMS messages.

A JMS session could be a locally transacted, non-transacted or distributed transacted.

28. What is JMS administered object?

JMS administered object is a pre-configured JMS object that is created by an administrator for the use of JMS clients and placed in JNDI namespace.

29. What is the difference between Bytes Message and Stream Message?

Bytes Message stores the primitive data types by converting them to their byte representation. Thus, the message is one contiguous stream of bytes. While the StreamMessage maintains a boundary between the different data types stored because it also stores the type information along with the value of the primitive being stored. Bytes Message allows data to be read using any type. Thus, even if your payload contains a long value, you can invoke a method to read a short and it will return you something. It will not give you a semantically correct data, but the call will succeed in reading the first two bytes of data. This is strictly prohibited in the StreamMessage.

30. How can asynchronous messaging deadlocks be avoided?

Asynchronous messages in JMS can be deadlocked if the close() method of a session is inside a user level synchronized block. To prevent these deadlock from occurring the user must specify the close() method outside of the area of the user-synchronized block.

31. What is the use of StreamMessage?

StreamMessage carries a stream of Java primitive types as it's payload. It contains some convenient methods for reading the data stored in the payload. However, StreamMessage prevents reading a long value as short, something that is allowed in case of BytesMessage. This is so because the StreamMessage also writes the type information alone with the value of the primitive type and enforces a set of strict conversion rules which prevents reading of one primitive type as another.

32. What is the use of ObjectMessage?

ObjectMessage contains a Serializable java object as it's payload. Thus, it allows exchange of Java objects between applications. This mandates that both the applications be Java applications. The consumer of the message must typecast the object received to it's appropriate type. Thus, the consumer should beforehand know the actual type of the object sent by the sender. Wrong type casting would result in ClassCastException.

Interview Q & A in JDBC

1.What is JDBC?

JDBC stands for Java Database Connectivity. It is an application program interface (API) specification for connecting programs written in Java to the data in popular databases.

2. What is a JDBC Driver?

JDBC driver is an interface enabling a Java application to interact with a database. To connect with individual databases, JDBC requires drivers for each database. The JDBC driver gives out the connection to the database and implements the protocol for transferring the query and result between client and database.

3. What is a connection?

Connection interface consists of methods for contacting a database. The connection object represents communication context.

4. What is the design pattern followed by JDBC?

JDBC architecture decouples an abstraction from its implementation. Hence JDBC follows a bridge design pattern. The JDBC API provides the abstraction and the JDBC drivers provide the implementation. New drivers can be plugged-in to the JDBC API without changing the client code.

5. What is difference between statement and prepared statement?

Prepared statements offer better performance, as they are pre-compiled. Prepared statements reuse the same execution plan for different arguments rather than creating a new execution plan every time. Prepared statements use bind arguments, which are sent to the database engine. This allows mapping different requests with same prepared statement but different arguments to execute the same execution plan. Prepared statements are more secure because they use bind variables, which can prevent SQL injection attack.

6. What does JDBC do?

JDBC can be used to perform the following functions:

Establishing connection with a database: It establishes the connection to the database that is used inside JAVA only and it allows the drivers to be defined such that it can be accessed from anywhere. The JDBC drivers are used for connectivity with other databases as well using the different methodology and functions.

Sending of SQL statements: This allow sending of queries and request to get the data from the database. The SQL statement provides a way to allow user in a convenient manner to produce the statements.

Processing of results: this allow easy processing of the result that is processed after getting the request from the client side.

7. What are the different types of drivers under JDBC?

There are four types of JDBC drivers which are as follows:

JDBC-ODBC bridge plus ODBC driver: It is responsible for providing access to JDBC via ODBC.

Native-API partly-Java driver: It is responsible for calling into client calls on API for difference system bases.

JDBC-Net pure Java driver: It is responsible for translating JDBC calls into DBMS net independent protocol which is further translated into DBMS protocol by a server.

Native-protocol pure Java driver: It is responsible for converting JDBC calls to network protocol which is used directly by DBMS.

8. What is the use of JDBC DriverManager class?

JDBC DriverManager is the factory class through which we get the Database Connection object. When we load the JDBC Driver class, it registers itself to the DriverManager, you can look up the JDBC Driver classes source code to check this.

Then when we call DriverManager.getConnection() method by passing the database configuration details, DriverManager uses the registered drivers to get the Connection and return it to the caller program.

9. Which type of JDBC driver is the fastest one?

Type 4 driver or Native-protocol, pure Java driver is the fastest driver because it converts the JDBC calls into vendor specific protocol calls which directly interacts with the database.

10. What are the types of statements in JDBC?

There are 3 JDBC statements.

Statement – used mostly for executing a static SQL statement at runtime. An object of Statement class can be created using Connection.createStatement() method.

PreparedStatement – used for executing same SQL statement multiple times. A SQL statement is pre-compiled and stored in a PreparedStatement object. This object can then be used to efficiently execute this statement multiple times. An object of PreparedStatement class can be created using Connection.prepareStatement() method.

CallableStatement – used to execute SQL stored procedures / functions. An object of CallableStatement class can be created using Connection.prepareCall() method.

11. What is the difference between preparedstatement and callablestatement?

PreparedStatement is used for executing a precompiled SQL statement multiple times. The CallableStatement is used to execute SQL stored procedures, Functions and cursors. CallableStatement extends the PreparedStatement Interface.

12. What are stored procedures? How to call stored procedure using JDBC API?

Stored procedure is a group of SQL statements that forms a logical unit and performs a task. The stored procedure is pre-compiled and stored in the database. Stored Procedures are used to encapsulate a set of operations or queries to execute on database. Stored procedures can be compiled and executed with different parameters and results and may have any combination of IN/OUT parameters. Stored procedures can be called using CallableStatement class in JDBC API.

13. How to invoke Oracle Stored Procedure with Database Objects as IN/OUT?

If Oracle Stored Procedure has IN/OUT parameters as DB Objects, then we need to create an Object array of the same size in the program and then use it to create Oracle STRUCT object. Then we can set this STRUCT object for the database object by calling setSTRUCT() method and work with it.

14. What is difference between java.util.Date and java.sql.Date?

java.util.Date contains information about the date and time whereas java.sql.Date contains information only about the date, it doesn't have time information. So, if you must keep time information in the database, it is advisable to use Timestamp or Date Time fields.

15. How do you register a driver?

There are 2 approaches for registering the Driver

Class.forName() – This method dynamically loads the driver's class file into memory, which automatically registers it. This method is preferable because it allows you to make the driver registration configurable and portable.

DriverManager.registerDriver() – This static method is used in case you are using a non-JDK compliant JVM, such as the one provided by Microsoft.

16. What are the common JDBC API components?

JDBC API consists of following interfaces and classes DriverManager, Driver, Connection, Statement, ResultSet, SQLException.

17. How can you determine whether a Statement and its ResultSet will be closed on a commit or rollback?

Use the DatabaseMetaData methods supportsOpenStatementsAcrossCommit() and supportsOpenStatementsAcrossRollback() to check.

If there is a practical limit for the number of SQL statements that can be added to an instance of a Statement object.

The specification makes no mention of any size limitation for Statement.addBatch(), this is dependent, on the driver.

18. How do you update a result set?

ResultSet interface contains a collection of update methods for updating the data of a result set. Each update method has two versions for each data type

One that takes in a column name.

One that takes in a column index.

These methods change the columns of the current row in the ResultSet object, but not in the underlying database. To update your changes to the row in the database, you need to invoke one of the following methods

updateRow(), deleteRow(), refreshRow(), cancelRowUpdates(), insertRow()

19. What is a ResultSet?

These objects hold data retrieved from a database after you execute an SQL query using Statement objects. It acts as an iterator to allow you to move through its data. The java.sql.ResultSet interface represents the result set of a database query.

20. How does JDBC handle the data types of Java and database?

The JDBC driver converts the Java data type to the appropriate JDBC type before sending it to the database. It uses a default mapping for most data types. For example, a Java int is converted to an SQL INTEGER.

21. What is the difference between execute, executeQuery, executeUpdate?

Boolean execute() - Executes the any kind of SQL statement.

ResultSet executeQuery() - This is used generally for reading the content of the database. The output will be in the form of ResultSet. Generally, SELECT statement is used.

int executeUpdate() - This is generally used for altering the databases. Generally, DROP TABLE or DATABASE, INSERT into TABLE, UPDATE TABLE, DELETE from TABLE statements will be used in this. The output will be in the form of int which denotes the number of rows affected by the query.

22. What is JDBC Batch Processing and what are its benefits?

Sometimes we need to run bulk queries of similar kind for a database, for example loading data from CSV files to relational database tables. As we know that we have option to use Statement or PreparedStatement to execute queries. Apart from that JDBC API provides Batch Processing feature through which we can execute bulk of queries in one go for a database.

JDBC API supports batch processing through Statement and PreparedStatement addBatch() and executeBatch() methods.

Batch Processing is faster than executing one statement at a time because the number of database calls are less.

23. What are common JDBC Exceptions?

Some of the common JDBC Exceptions are:

java.sql. SQLException – This is the base exception class for JDBC exceptions.

java.sql.BatchUpdateException – This exception is thrown when Batch operation fails, but it depends on the JDBC driver whether they throw this exception or the base SQLException.

java.sql.SQLWarning – For warning messages in SQL operations.

java.sql.DataTruncation – when a data values is unexpectedly truncated for reasons other than its having exceeded MaxFieldSize.

24. What is SQL Warning? How to retrieve SQL warnings in the JDBC program?

SQLWarning is the subclass of SQLException and we can retrieve it by calling getWarnings() method on Connection, Statement, and ResultSet objects. SQL Warnings doesn't stop the execution of the script but alerts the user about the warning.

25. What causes "No suitable driver" error?

"No suitable driver" is occurs during a call to the DriverManager.getConnection method, may be of any of the following reason

Due to failing to load the appropriate JDBC drivers before calling the getConnection method.

It can be specifying an invalid JDBC URL, one that is not recognized by JDBC driver.

This error can occur if one or more the shared libraries needed by the bridge cannot be loaded.

26. Why Prepared Statements are faster?

Prepared execution is faster than direct execution for statements executed more than three or four times because the statement is compiled only once. Prepared statements and JDBC driver are linked with each other. We can bind drivers with columns by triggering the query into the database. When we execute Connection.prepareStatement(), all the columns bindings take place, to reduce the time.

27. What are DML and DDL?

Data Manipulation Language (DDL) this portion of the SQL standard is concerned with manipulating the data in a database as opposed to the structure of a database. The DML deals with the SELECT, INSERT, DELETE, UPDATE, COMMIT and ROLLBACK.

Data Definition Language (DDL) this portion of the SQL standard is concerned with the creation, deletion and modification of database objects like tables, indexes and views. The core verbs for DDL are CREATE, ALTER and DROP. While most DBMS engines allow DDL to be used dynamically, it is often not supported in transactions.

28. What are the three parts of a JDBC URL?

A JDBC URL consists of three parts, which are separated by colons:

1. Protocol: It is always JDBC.

2. Subprotocol: It is the mechanism of driver or database connectivity which might be supported by 1 or more drivers. Example of a sub-protocol name is ODBC, to access a database through a JDBC-ODBC bridge, one might use a URL such as the following:

jdbc:odbc:sid

In this example, the sub-protocol is ODBC, and the sub-name sid is a local ODBC data source.

3. Sub-name: It is the way by which database is identified. It can vary and have sub name depending on the protocol.

29. How to rollback a JDBC transaction?

We can use Connection object rollback() method to rollback the transaction. It will rollback all the changes made by the transaction and release any database locks currently held by this Connection object.

30. What is 2 phase commits?

When we work in distributed systems where multiple databases are involved, we are required to use 2 phase commit protocol. 2 phase commit protocol is an atomic commitment protocol for distributed systems. In the first phase, transaction manager sends commit-request to all the transaction resources. If all the transaction resources are OK, then transaction manager commits the transaction changes for all the resources. If any of the transaction resource responds as Abort, then the transaction manager can rollback all the transaction changes.

31.How do I insert an image file (or other raw data) into a database?

All raw data types should be read and uploaded to the database as an array of bytes, byte [].

Originating from a binary file.

Read all data from the file using a FileInputStream.

Create a byte array from the read data.

Use method setBytes(int index, byte [] data); of java.sql.PreparedStatement to upload the data.

32. Differentiate between a Statement and a PreparedStatement.

A standard Statement is used for creating a Java representation for a literal SQL statement and for executing it on the database.

A PreparedStatement is a precompiled Statement.

A Statement must verify its metadata in the database every time.

But, the PreparedStatement must verify its metadata in the database only once.

If we execute the SQL statement, it will go to the STATEMENT.

But, if we want to execute a single SQL statement for the multiple number of times, it'll go to the PreparedStatement.

33.How are PL/SQL stored procedures called from the JDBC programs by creating the prepareCall() in the Connection object.

A call to the method prepareCall() carries out variable bind parameters as input parameters, output variables & makes an object instance of the CallableStatement class.

The following line of code implies this:

Callable Statement stproc_ stmt = conn.prepareCall("{call procname(?,?,?)}");

where conn is the instance of the Connection class.

34. Explain the two tiers and three tier architectures of JDBC.

Two tiers and three tiers are structures supported by JDBC API info accessing database. The Java applet can directly interact with the database with help of JDBC driver which can communicate with data base management system which is being accessed under the two-tier model. Under three tier model the middle tier gets a role to play. Commands are forwarded to SQL statements via the middle tier. Then the SQL statement is processes by the database and sent to user via the middle tier again.

35. What is an escape syntax?

Escape syntax is used for signaling the driver that the code within it should be handled differently. The escape clause is demarcated by curly braces and a key word:
{keyword . . . parameters . . .}

36. What is pessimistic concurrency?

Pessimistic concurrency is used to lock the resources required for the time span of a transaction's execution. In this mode, the lock on the record is held until the edit duration is completed. No user can get a lock on the same record for updating. A transaction is assured of successful completion, unlike dead locks.

37. What is Optimistic Locking?

Optimistic Locking locks the record only when updating takes place. It ensures that the locks are held between selecting, updating, or deleting rows. This process needs a way to ensure that the changes to data are not performed between the time of being read and being altered. The primary advantage of optimistic locking is, it minimizes the time for which a given resource is unavailable which is used by another transaction and in this way, it more scalable locking alternative.

38. What is a "dirty read"?

- In typical database transactions, one transaction reads change the value while the other reads the value before committing or rolling back by the first transaction. This reading process is called as 'dirty read'.

Because there is always a chance that the first transaction might rollback the change which causes the second transaction reads an invalid value.

- It takes no notice of any other lock taken by another process.

- It is a problem if the uncommitted transaction fails or is rolled back.

39. What is cold backup, hot backup, warm backup recovery?

- Cold backup is a recovery technique, in which the files must be backed up before the database is restarted at the same time.

- Hot backup is a recovery technique for each table space and is taken at the time of accessing and running the database.

- Warm back is a recovery technique where all the tables are locked, and users cannot access at the time of backing up data. The backup operations can be postponed in case the users are accessing the database.

40. What is PreparedStatement?

PreparedStatement is called as “pre-compiled statement”. An SQL statement is compiled beforehand and stored in the PreparedStatement object. The purpose of precompiled statement is that the statement can be executed repeatedly. The required parameter values are to be substituted from time to time.

41. What is the advantage of using a PreparedStatement?

A PreparedStatement Object would be faster than a Statement Object where repeated execution of SQL statements is required. The reason is that the creation of a PreparedStatement object causes it to be precompiled within the database. So, it does not have to be recompiled during the execution again and again.

Usually, these objects are used when SQL statements take parameters.

42. What are the standard isolation levels defined by JDBC?

The standard isolation levels are

transaction_none

transaction_read_committed

transaction_read_uncommitted

transaction_repeatable_read

transaction_serializable

43. What is SavePoint?

A savepoint marks a point that the current transaction can roll back to. Instead of rolling all its changes back, it can choose to roll back only some of them. For example, suppose you

start a transaction.

insert 10 rows into a table.

set a savepoint.

insert another 5 rows.

rollback to the savepoint.

commit the transaction.

After doing this, the table will contain the first 10 rows you inserted. The other 5 rows will have been deleted by the rollback. A savepoint is just a marker that the current transaction can roll back to.

44. What is JDBC ResultSet?

JDBC ResultSet is like a table of data representing a database result set, which is usually generated by executing a statement that queries the database.

ResultSet object maintains a cursor pointing to its current row of data. Initially the cursor is positioned before the first row. The next() method moves the cursor to the next row. If there are no more rows, next() method returns false and it can be used in a while loop to iterate through the result set.

A default ResultSet object is not updatable and has a cursor that moves forward only. Thus, you can iterate through it only once and only from the first row to the last row.

45. What are different types of ResultSet?

There are different types of ResultSet objects that we can get based on the user input while creating the Statement. If you will investigate the Connection methods, you will see that createStatement() and prepareStatement() method are overloaded to provide ResultSet type and concurrency as input argument.

There are three types of ResultSet object.

ResultSet.type_forward_only: This is the default type and cursor can only move forward in the result set.

ResultSet.type_scroll_insensitive: The cursor can move forward and backward, and the result set is not sensitive to changes made by others to the database after the result set was created.

ResultSet.type_scroll_sensitive: The cursor can move forward and backward, and the result set is sensitive to changes made by others to the database after the result set was created.

Based on the concurrency there are two types of ResultSet object.

ResultSet.concur_read_only: The result set is read only, this is the default concurrency type.

ResultSet.concur_updatable: We can use ResultSet update method to update the rows data.

46. What is JDBC RowSet?

JDBC RowSet holds tabular data in more flexible ways that ResultSet. All RowSet objects are derived from ResultSet, so they have all the capabilities of ResultSet with some additional features. RowSet interface is defined in javax.sql package.

47. What are different types of RowSet?

RowSet are broadly divided into two types:

Connected RowSet Objects – These objects are connected to database and are most like ResultSet object. JDBC API provides only one connected RowSet object javax.sql.rowset.JdbcRowSet and its standard implementation class is com.sun.rowset.JdbcRowSetImpl

Disconnected RowSet Objects – These RowSet objects are not required to connected to a database, so they are more lightweight and serializable. They are suitable for sending data over a network.

48. Explain different type of disconnected row set?

There are four types of disconnected RowSet implementations.

CachedRowSet – They can get the connection and execute a query and read the ResultSet data to populate the RowSet data. We can manipulate and update data while it is disconnected and reconnect to database and write the changes.

WebRowSet derived from CachedRowSet – They can read and write XML document.

JoinRowSet derived from WebRowSet – They can form SQL JOIN without having to connect to a data source.

FilteredRowSet derived from WebRowSet – We can apply filtering criteria so that only selected data is visible.

49. What is the difference between ResultSet and RowSet?

RowSet objects are derived from ResultSet, so they have all the features of ResultSet with some additional features. One of the huge benefit of RowSet is that they can be disconnected and that makes it lightweight and easy to transfer over a network.

Whether to use ResultSet or RowSet depends on your requirements but if you are planning to use ResultSet for longer duration, then a disconnected RowSet is better choice to free database resources.

50. What is database connection pooling? What are the advantages of using a connection pool?

Connection pooling is the mechanism by which we reuse connection objects which are used to make connection with the database. It allows multiple clients to share a cached set of connection objects. Getting connection and disconnecting are costly operation, which can affect the application performance, so we should avoid creating multiple connection objects during multiple database interactions.

A pool contains set of database connection objects which are already connected to the database, and any client who wants to use it can take it from pool and it can be returned to the pool when done with using.

Apart from performance this also saves you resources as there may be limited database connections available for your application.

****

Interview Q & A in JNDI

1.What Is Jndi?

JNDI stands for Java Naming and Directory Interface. It provides a generic interface to LDAP (Lightweight Directory Access Protocol) and other directory services like NDS, DNS (Domain Name System) etc. It provides a means for an application to locate components that exist in a name space according to certain attributes.

2.What are the components of JNDI?

Components of JNDI

Naming Interface- The naming interface organizes information hierarchically and maps human-friendly names to addresses or objects that are machine-friendly. It allows access to named objects through multiple namespaces.

Directory Interface- JNDI includes a directory service interface that provides access to directory objects, which can contain attributes, thereby providing attribute-based searching and schema support

Service Provider Interface- JNDI comes with the SPI, which supports the protocols provided by third parties.

3.Which protocols JNDI supports?

JNDI supports popular protocols, such as LDAP (Lightweight Directory Access Protocol), NDS (Netscape Directory Service), DNS (Domain Naming Service), and NIS (Network Information Service), supplied by different vendors.

4. What is JNDI naming service?

A naming service maintains a set of bindings. Bindings maps names to objects. All objects in a naming system are named in the same way and follow the same naming convention. Clients use the naming service to locate objects by name.

5. What is JNDI Lookup?

lookup() attempts to find the specified object in the given context. It looks for a single, specific object and either finds it in the current JNDI context or it fails.

6.What is the importance of JNDI?

To centralize the information storage the enterprises uses LDAP. The information is of user names, passwords, email addresses, printers, determination of database access. Multiple database management is reduced by centralizing the information.

7. What is a Jndi Initialcontext ?

All naming operations are relative to a context. The InitalContext implements the Context interface and provides an entry point for the resolution of names.

8. What's the difference between JNDI lookup (), list (), listBindings (), and search ()?

lookup() attempts to find the specified object in the given context. I.e., it looks for a single, specific object and either finds it in the current context or it fails.

list() attempts to return an enumeration of all the NameClassPair's of all the objects in the current context. I.e., it's a listing of all the objects in the current context but only returns the object's name and the name of the class to which the object belongs.

listBindings() attempts to return an enumeration of the Bindings of all the objects in the current context. I.e., it's a listing of all the objects in the current context with the object's name, its class name, and a reference to the object itself.

search() attempts to return an enumeration of all the objects matching a given set of search criteria. It can search across multiple contexts (or not). It can return whatever attributes of the objects that you desire. Etc. It's by far the most complex and powerful of these options but is also the most expensive.

9. What is a Directory Service?

Searching for files and directories done by providing Directory services. A directory service is a set of names. The user and resource information and machine addresses are summarized by directory service. For example, for a given user name, the service returns the attributes of the user such as telephone no, email address etc. A directory service uses the databases that specialized and hierarchical in design.

10. Difference between JNDI list and listBindings method.

list() attempts to return an enumeration of all the objects in the current context as NameClassPair.

listBindings() attempts to return an enumeration of all the object bindings in the current context.

11. What is LDAP?

Lightweight Directory Access Protocol (LDAP) is a protocol for locating organizations, individuals, and other resources such as files and devices in a network, whether on the public Internet or on a corporate intranet.

12. How does JNDI relate to LDAP?

JNDI provides an excellent object-oriented abstraction of directory and naming. Developers using JNDI can produce queries that use LDAP or other access protocols to retrieve results.

13. Why do we need JNDI when communication using LDAP is possible?

JNDI provides lookup of resources like a database or a message queue enabling a uniform way to access directory services.

14. What is the main package of JNDI API.

javax.naming package.

15 How does JNDI relate to Netscape's Java LDAP API?

Netscape's API is LDAP-specific. It is used for low-level access to LDAP directories. It exposes details about the protocol that applications typically do not need to know.

16.How does JNDI relate to OMG's CORBA standards for naming?

A Java CORBA application can use JNDI to access to the CORBA (COS) name service, as well as other naming and directory services.

It offers the application one interface for accessing all these naming and directory services.

Using JNDI also paves the way for Java CORBA applications to use a distributed enterprise-level service like LDAP to store object references.

17. How does JNDI relate to Microsoft's ADSI?

The Java ADSI package allows Java programs to access Active Directory based on the COM model.

Although it can be used to access other directories, it is a Windows-centric solution.

JNDI offers Java applications, regardless of whether they're running on Windows or accessing Active Directory, to access directories using the Java object model.

For example, you can manipulate objects such as AWT and JavaBeans components, bind them into the directory, and look them back up without having to do any translation or deal with data representation issues.

18. What is XFN and how does this relate to JNDI?

XFN is X/Open Federated Naming, a C-based standard for accessing multiple, possibly federated naming and directory services.
A programmer familiar with XFN will find it easy to use JNDI.

19. Who Should Use Jndi?

Any Java application that needs to access information about users, machines, networks, and services. User information includes security credentials, phone numbers, electronic and postal mail addresses, and application preferences. Machine information includes network addresses, machine configurations, etc. In addition, any Java application that needs to either export objects or access objects exported by other applications and services. Examples include printers, calendars, and networked file systems.

20. What is Context and InitialContext?

Answer: A context represents a set of bindings within a naming service. A Context object provides the methods for binding names to objects and unbinding names from objects, for renaming objects, and for listing the bindings. JNDI performs all naming operations relative to a context.

The JNDI specification defines an InitialContext class. This class is instantiated with properties that define the type of naming service in use (such as provider URL, security, ID and password to use when connecting).

21.Does JNDI support Security?

Yes. JNDI allows for applications to work in conjunction with directory-specific security systems.

****

****

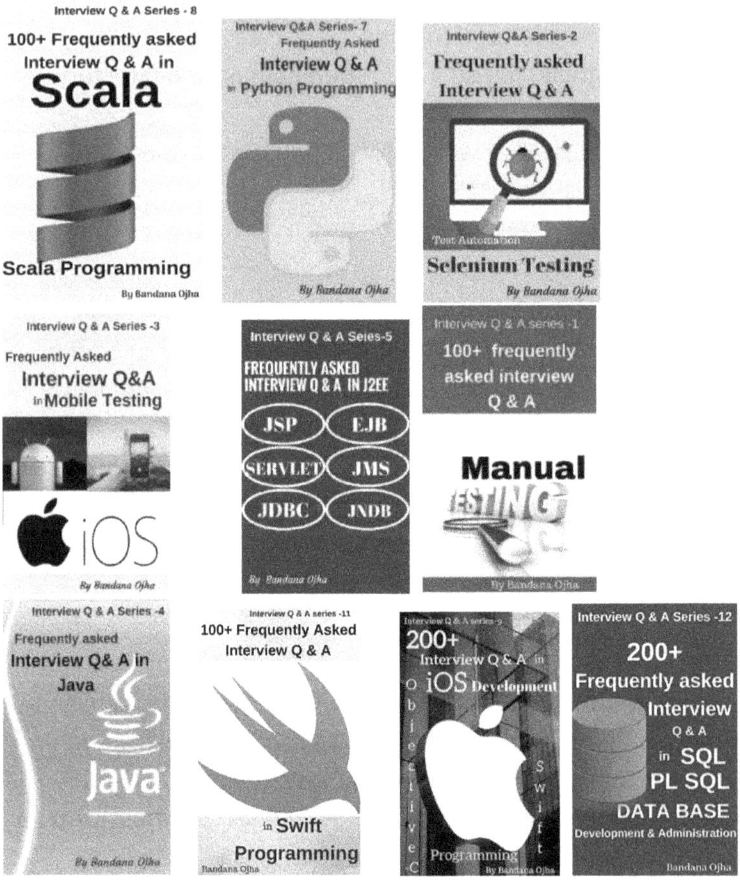

www.ingramcontent.com/pod-product-compliance
Lightning Source LLC
LaVergne TN
LVHW092337060326
832902LV00008B/689

* 9 7 8 1 9 8 0 2 8 1 2 6 9 *